THE EXTRAORDINARY LIFE OF CHARLES DICKENS

CHARLES DICKENS

The Extraordinary Life of Charles Dickens

AN EXHIBITION AT THE GROLIER CLUB

OF NEW YORK

CURATED BY

Ralph J. Crawford, Jr.

AND

Bruce J. Crawford

THE GROLIER CLUB · NEW YORK

2006

CATALOGUE OF AN EXHIBITION

HELD AT THE GROLIER CLUB

26 JANUARY – 10 MARCH 2006

To All Dickensians
Past, Present, and Future

CONTENTS

INTRODUCTION

John Patterson and the Dickens Archive

Judge John Patterson – the first compiler of these autograph letters, portraits, part-covers and illustrations – was an avid Dickens enthusiast. He served as president of the Philadelphia branch of the Dickens Fellowship and was a member of the Grolier Club from 1921 until his death in 1925.

Patterson's close friend John C. Eckel was the author of *The First Editions of the Writings of Charles Dickens and Their Values,* the 1913 bibliography which Patterson hoped to extra-illustrate with his material. Eckel was a member of the Grolier Club from 1918 until 1937.

After Judge Patterson's untimely death in 1925, his archive remained in Sessler's Bookshop in Philadelphia. Over time, its purpose was forgotten, as it remained boxed up and undisturbed in the shop. In 1963, the archive became part of Ralph Crawford's library.

Now, more than eighty years after Patterson's death, his archive is being exhibited for the first time. Rather than being used for its original purpose of extra-illustrating the bibliography of Dickens, these items form the basis for illustrating Dickens's relationships with family members, friends, and professional associates, and with the British and American public.

Patterson and his Friendships with Fellow Dickensians

In 1913, the same year that saw John Patterson's appointment to the Common Pleas Court, Chapman and Hall of London published John C. Eckel's landmark bibliography, *The First Editions of the Writings of Charles Dickens and Their Values.* Eckel's work succeeded, for the first time, in providing notable advances in the Dickens scholarly canon, including detailed collations of Dickens's first editions; reproductions of variant issue "points"; and a fascinating chapter devoted to Dickens presentation copies and their values. As Eckel says in his introduction, "... Dickens essentially is a collector's author, for the reason that his books in their original state make an irresistible appeal."

Eckel dedicated his *Bibliography,* which remains today a standard reference for Dickens collectors, "To Those Collectors of Fine and Rare Books Who Include Charles Dickens Among Their Favorite Authors." John Patterson was certainly one of those collectors whom Eckel had in mind. The noted bookman and author A. Edward Newton describes a convivial meeting between Eckel, Patterson, collector William Elkins, and himself. In *The Greatest Book in the World,* Newton describes Patterson's achievements as a collector of Dickens:

> ... it would be fatiguing to refer to the items in Mr. Elkins's collection; let me say, in a word, that he has what is generally regarded as the finest Dickens collection in the world. There was, too, Judge John M. Patterson, President of the Dickens Fellowship, whose knowledge of first editions is exceeded only by that of another of the group, Mr. John C. Eckel, the author of a *Bibliography* of Dickens, as readable as it is accurate. There was also the writer of this paper, resembling in appearance, it is said, Mr. Pickwick himself, badly distanced in the race as a collector by these other men either longer of purse or fleeter of foot than he.

Clearly, Patterson was active and dedicated in his enthusiasm for Dickens, and in his friendships with fellow collectors, book dealers and scholars. On April 29, 1914, in an effort to aid the Samaritan, Children's Homeopathic, St. Agnes and Mt. Sinai Hospitals, he performed on stage at the Academy of Music in Philadelphia in the *Mock Trial of John Jasper for the Murder of Edwin Drood.* John C. Eckel, William Elkins, the booksellers A. S. W. Rosenbach and Charles Sessler, and others also acted in the mock trial.

The resulting limited-edition publication of the trial performance script, edited by Patterson, is one of the works sought by Dickens collectors today as an important sequel to *Edwin Drood.* Interestingly enough, and counter to the conclusions drawn by the majority of sequels addressing the Drood murder case, Jasper was acquitted at the end of the 1914 charity performance.

Development of the Patterson Archive

At some point shortly after the publication in 1913 of the Eckel *Bibliography*, Patterson resolved to undertake a most extraordinary and ambitious project: the assembly of a remarkable archive of material that would extra-illustrate Eckel's work.

Extra-illustration was a frequent – even commonplace – undertaking for enthusiastic collectors and bibliophiles in the early twentieth century. But Patterson must have decided that his effort would be unique, and would culminate in the production of a group of volumes superior to any other extra-illustrated work that had yet been assembled.

To this end, he chose to collect manuscript material, principally in the form of original letters, written by the authors, illustrators, publishers, and theatrical performers mentioned in the pages of the Eckel *Bibliography*. In his enthusiasm for original printed material that would show off the details of variant issues, Patterson added to his growing archive many examples of these points from original editions of Dickens. Patterson also assembled: portraits of many associates of Dickens mentioned by Eckel; numerous original cover sheets for the serial appearances of Dickens's works; examples of the plates that illustrated Dickens first editions; and rare related ephemeral material. Patterson pushed onward by adding contemporary advertising and newspaper material announcing the 1913 publication of the *Bibliography*. In all, John Patterson gathered together over 400 individual items, including 90 original manuscript pieces, all of which were presumably to be included in the extra-illustrated *Bibliography*.

Patterson must have known that in order to assemble a collection of material that would meet his ambitious objectives, he needed help to find source material, as well as access to informed colleagues who could provide scholarly advice. Patterson found that help and access at Charles Sessler's bookshop in Philadelphia. A prominent dealer,

Sessler specialized in Dickens, as well as in illustrated books. Sessler was instrumental in founding the Philadelphia branch of the Dickens Fellowship. A. Edward Newton said of him in *The Amenities of Book-Collecting:* "[He] had some unexpectedly fine things from time to time. He goes abroad every year with his pocket full of money, and comes back with a lot of things that quickly empty ours. Dickens is one of his specialties. . . . Sessler studies his customer's weaknesses – that's where his strength lies."

From the standpoint of being able to locate the material he needed in extra-illustrating the *Bibliography,* Sessler's Bookshop was the perfect locale. Sessler had in stock, or could (and did) obtain multiple, disbound, broken, and incomplete copies of Dickens's works as well as related ephemeral material. Patterson undoubtedly chose items from this extensive inventory. While it would be anathema to modern-day collectors, the practice of gathering extra-illustration material in this manner was nonetheless common practice in the early twentieth century.

Mabel Zahn, the manager of the rare book department at Sessler's, partly corroborated this account of Patterson's activities. She remembered in 1963 that Patterson had worked directly out of the shop in an attempt to complete a Dickens project. Strangely, while also a Dickens enthusiast and expert, she had no more specific knowledge then of what Patterson was trying to achieve. That said, Patterson had nonetheless come remarkably close to achieving his goal: he had reached the point of carefully mounting all of his gathered material on thick paper, selected in part to be compatible with the size of the sheets used in printing the large-paper edition of the Dickens *Bibliography.*

After Patterson died suddenly in 1925, the material remained with Sessler's until 1963. Ralph Crawford, who had purchased some rare books from Ms. Zahn at Sessler's and who was an enthusiastic Dickensian at the time, was offered the Patterson archive for a nominal price. He accepted.

The disorganized archive resisted more modern interpretation for a time. But in the process of sorting the material, Crawford discovered that Patterson's penciled numberings on each individual leaf referred to corresponding pages in the Eckel *Bibliography*! Each archive item was to illustrate a specific entry in Eckel's book. The archive's code had been broken.

Interpreting the Archive for the Exhibition

Eighty years after Patterson's work was left uncompleted, it is impossible to know the exact nature of his ambition. We can, of course, speculate. He may have wanted to produce a very beautiful and unique book. He may have wanted to add in a definitive way to the legacies of Dickens and Eckel, and perhaps memorialize himself in the effort. He may have used the project to prove his own resourcefulness, tenacity and scholarship. Patterson may have been inspired by the Grolier Club's Dickens exhibition in 1913, where bibliographical issue points and variants were displayed together, some for the first time. He may have operated with a simple obsession: to obtain an item that corresponded to every significant mention by Eckel, in the *Bibliography*, of a person, place name, or subtle issue point.

Through his selection of material, Patterson created the foundation for rich pictures of Dickens's relationships with contemporaries. Seen through the archive are the novelist's tempestuous interactions with publishers; his emotional devotion to Mary Hogarth, the younger sister of his wife Catherine; and his rejection of the religious tenets of the Church of England (in which he had been brought up) in favor of Unitarian principles.

The discerning exhibition visitor will notice that the archive contains substantial groups of items related to the *Pickwick Papers* (interesting from a bibliographic point of view) and to the five Christmas books (with a focus on the life and work of their illustrators). Patterson's appreciation for bibliography, and his love of Dickens's passion for Christmas, may explain this concentration of material.

The Eckel *Bibliography* and the Patterson archive also contain many items relating to stage productions in which Dickens participated as author, director, producer, and/or actor, and to his involvement with various literary periodicals such as *Household Words, All the Year Round,* and *The Gad's Hill Gazette.* Without doubt, these concentrations of material are appropriate, as the theater and periodical journalism played large and influential parts in Dickens's life and work.

Certainly of prime significance is the material that serves to illuminate Dickens's complex and often surprising relations with family members, friends, literary associates, and with the British and American public. Dickens's rapid rise to popularity, beginning with the serial appearance of *Pickwick Papers,* and sustained throughout his life, is bound inextricably to his obsession with social reform and his support for London's poor and disadvantaged. His popularity is also bound to his love of showmanship and the stage, and to his relentless pursuit of his own fame and fortune. Whatever individual conclusions may be drawn about Dickens, the Patterson archive reaches beyond them to reveal a life truly extraordinary in its richness, complexity, and genius.

JOHN M. PATTERSON:
A SHORT RETROSPECTIVE

John M. Patterson was born in Philadelphia on March 4, 1874. After attending public schools, he took at the age of 14 a position in a stockbroker's office earning $2.50 a week, and subsequently he clerked for the Pennsylvania Railroad. Deciding to study law, Patterson attended preparatory school and was subsequently admitted to law school at the University of Pennsylvania. There, the study of law required three years, but Patterson completed his work in two, applied to the courts to take the bar examination, and passed. During the Spanish-American War, Patterson enlisted as a color sergeant in the First Pennsylvania Volunteers. Before leaving the service, he rose to the rank of captain in command of Company L, 19th Regiment. In 1902, while practicing law, Patterson was appointed assistant city solicitor.

As a young man, Patterson was fond of athletics. As a member of the Vesper boat club, he was a skilled oarsman. His strength of character was demonstrated dramatically in the summer of 1903, when he leaped from an Atlantic City pier, fully clothed except for his overcoat, and saved the life of an exhausted swimmer. A Philadelphia newspaper reported that, when asked about this event, Patterson said: "Oh, what's the use of trying to make a hero of me . . . the man was not drowning. All he wanted was company in the water, as he had lost his head." In 1909, in another act of bravery, Patterson entered a burning building in Philadelphia, climbed to the third story, and carried an endangered child to safety.

No doubt due to Patterson's intelligence and strength of character, his legal career progressed rapidly. After having been appointed assistant district attorney in 1904, he was appointed in June 1913 to fill a vacancy in the Common Pleas Court No. 1. In this position, Patterson carried on a distinguished public service career and was often cited in the Philadelphia press for landmark legal decisions.

In 1917, when the United States entered World War I, Patterson was one of the first volunteers to offer his services to Theodore Roosevelt, when the colonel announced his plans to form the "Roosevelt Division," a cavalry unit, and take this division to France. Roosevelt was denied permission from the government, and Patterson, then in his forties, did not serve. However, Patterson did use his enormous popularity and public presence to speak out on behalf of the recruitment and volunteer efforts.

In 1919, John Patterson had a political setback: he was unsuccessful as a candidate for the Republican nomination for mayor, losing by the tiny margin of just over 1300 votes. He continued his legal career, and then in the spring of 1922, retired from the bench and re-entered private practice. Public speculation at the time treated his unexpected retirement as motivated by Patterson's wish to build a personal fortune, since he had suffered under the relatively lower pay of public service.

In 1925, Patterson again moved toward public service: he ran on the Republican ticket for district attorney of Philadelphia. In late October, as the election approached, he was quietly admitted to Lankenau Hospital and underwent surgery for gallstone colic, from which he had suffered for several years. On October 30 he was pronounced out of all danger and recovering well, but his health suddenly worsened, and he died from complications on November 3, at the age of 51, four hours after winning the election.

Patterson was survived by his wife Edna, daughters Marie Louise and Helen India, and infant granddaughter Patricia. Some newspapers reported that 100,000 people came to pay their respects in advance of his funeral.

Judge Patterson's legal career paralleled a lifelong devotion to charitable and social works. He served as trustee of Temple University, Garretson Hospital, and Samaritan Hospital. He was a director of

Maternity Hospital. In 1921, Patterson dressed as Santa Claus and distributed 2000 baskets of "Christmas cheer" to families of prisoners in local jails. On the occasion of his sixteenth wedding anniversary, Patterson took 700 youngsters from poorer sections of Philadelphia on an all-day outing to Neshaminy Falls. In May 1922, Patterson sold a portion of his library in New York to raise much-needed funds. His many friends, upon hearing of the sale, arranged for a testimonial dinner, at which $5000 was pledged to enable Patterson to purchase a new library. Patterson refused the gift, and requested that the funds be distributed among various charitable institutions. In June 1922, Patterson was elevated by the King of Italy to chevalier of the Order of the Crown of Italy.

While professional success and charitable endeavor figured prominently in Judge Patterson's life, he also displayed a passionate love for books and book collecting. His love was an active one, as he served as both president and vice president of the Philadelphia branch of the Dickens Fellowship, and was elected to the Grolier Club of New York in 1921.

The *Philadelphia Public Ledger* for Sunday morning, January 9, 1916 ran an important article written by journalist Joseph Jackson, who had interviewed Patterson on the subject of his library. In it, Patterson revealed to Jackson much about his love for books, which he had been collecting for twenty years, and about his library, which then held 10,000 volumes. Jackson wrote:

> He [Patterson] told me how he had contrived to gather so many interesting books and relics, for his library contains a large number of interesting autograph letters of persons of prominence either in the literary world or in history... They have been gathered from everywhere books are sold, from visits to bookstores in this country and in England, from catalogs from various parts of the world and from auction. . . . Becoming interested in Dickens, first in his works, then in his career, the Judge started to collect first editions of the novelist.

Jackson continued: "In answer to my question as to his reason for having his library in three places, the Judge replied that he liked to have his books with him. 'It might be inconvenient were it not that I have a large part of my Dickens collection always at hand so I can use it when getting up material for Dickens papers for the Fellowship.'"

Jackson and other journalists also documented a Patterson library that reached well beyond Charles Dickens. As a lifelong resident of Philadelphia, with a keen interest in Philadelphia history, Patterson acquired William Penn's copy of the Bible, inscribed by Penn to his son. Among other association items in the Patterson collection was the door knocker from Dr. Johnson's house in Gough Square. Patterson also had a second folio Shakespeare, a leaf from the Gutenberg Bible, first editions of *Robinson Crusoe* and *The Vicar of Wakefield,* and a 27-line fragment on vellum of *Donatus.* When Jackson asked Patterson if he had moved on from collecting Dickens, he said he had, as there appeared to be nothing more left of the great novelist for him to collect! Patterson showed off his most valuable Dickens book, a first issue of *Oliver Twist* inscribed by Dickens to his friend Serjeant Talfourd, the dedicatee of *Pickwick Papers.*

Eight years after Jackson's newspaper article appeared, Patterson was interviewed again, in December 1924 and in the last year of his life. When the journalist asked about Dickens and Christmas, Patterson replied:

> Dickens has been called the "Great Heart of Bookland"... Thackeray called him the Christmas prophet. Of one thing it is certain, however. He understood the spirit of the time as no other man ever has done....
>
> Alive to all its beauty, susceptible and responsive to all its suggestions and romance, he [Dickens] reveled in it with all the breathless interest and intensity of a child....
>
> He caught its mystery, and his heart throbbed with its poetry.

Patterson, touched by the artistic vibrancy of Dickens, had collected what pleased him.

THREE GENERATIONS OF
COLLECTING

___

*T*he *Extraordinary Life of Charles Dickens* exhibit, web site and book have been collaborative efforts of father and son, Ralph Jay Crawford, Jr. and Bruce Jay Crawford.

Inspirations for this Exhibition

Three important considerations guided Ralph and Bruce Crawford's proposal to mount this Grolier Club exhibition.

- The first was to present a collection rich with ephemeral material, for an exhibit that would be visually appealing and that could be developed into a narrative about an author's life and writings.

- The second consideration was to present material which had a special connection to the Grolier Club.

- Last, and partly at the suggestion of Eric Holzenberg, was to apply technology to extend the range and breadth of the exhibit.

As a result of these considerations, Ralph and Bruce proposed *The Extraordinary Life of Charles Dickens,* based on the Patterson archive of Dickens material. To permit web users to browse the Patterson archive they created the web site: www.charlesdickensonline.com.

At the time this volume went to press, web site visitors were recorded from the following locations: Australia, Belgium, Brazil, Canada, Chile, China, Colombia, Czech Republic, Dubai, France, Germany, India, Italy, Japan, Jordan, Mexico, Netherlands, Poland, Romania, Russia, Seychelles Islands, Slovak Republic, South Africa, South Korea, Switzerland, Taiwan, and the United Kingdom.

Ralph Crawford's Comments on a Collecting Family

I became a rare-book collector in 1953 when I began collecting material relating to Charles Dickens. My first purchase was the *Mystery of Edwin Drood* in the original parts, purchased from Dawson's Book Shop in Los Angeles.

I expanded my collecting interests in the next decade to include the writings of Anthony Trollope and Sir Walter Scott. I was advised by a prominent Pasadena book dealer to "collect high points" if I wished to maximize long-term appreciation in the value of antiquarian books, and was offered from the dealer's stock Defoe's *Robinson Crusoe*, Keats's *Lamia*, and Gibbon's *Decline and Fall of the Roman Empire*. With a limited purse, I recognized that I would only be able to afford one or two high points per year and would have to forego the pleasures of "the hunt." I ignored the dealer's high-point advice and purchased a copy of Anthony Trollope's *Last Chronicle of Barset* instead.

Over the years, I have collected a large number of English and American authors and poets, from Matthew Prior to Robert Frost. I have continued to collect Dickens in depth, concentrating especially on theatrical and musical adaptations of Dickens's work.

My son, Grolier Club member Bruce Crawford, was nine when he bought his first rare book in 1963. It was a first edition of *Lives of the Hunted* by Ernest Seton-Thompson, the artist-naturalist, and it was purchased from Holmes Book Store in Oakland, California. In his early teens, Bruce expanded his collecting interests to include John Buchan's *The Thirty-Nine Steps, Greenmantle*, and other adventure stories.

My father (Ralph Crawford, Sr.) was also interested in collecting. He was a friend of Russ Kingman, an authority on Jack London and the owner of a large archive of material concerning the author. My father, a longtime Oakland resident, developed an interest in early California history books as well as in Jack London and London-ana. Oakland, California was the locale of many of London's exploits and is the setting of his adventures as an oyster pirate, as related in *The Cruise of the Dazzler*. My father gave Bruce his Jack London collection when Bruce was in his early twenties, and Bruce continued to broaden and deepen this collection. In 2002, Bruce exhibited an early manuscript poem by Jack London as part of an exhibition titled *The Grolier Club Collects*.

Bruce did follow the "high points" route for a time during the 1970s, collecting Sterne's *Tristram Shandy,* Fielding's *Tom Jones,* Johnson's *Dictionary,* and Brontë's *Jane Eyre.* However, Bruce now collects a range of English and American authors in depth, from John Milton, and early seventeenth-century playwrights, to Lafcadio Hearn. Bruce's primary collecting interest continues to be William Makepeace Thackeray, emphasizing Thackeray's work as an illustrator.

Warren Howell of John Howell Books in San Francisco was an early influence on our collecting strategies. He was fond of telling collectors: "Collect what pleases you. It doesn't matter whether others think it's important or not. If it pleases you, collect it." Bruce and I have followed Warren Howell's advice in assembling our literary collections. In addition to authors' published works, ephemeral material such as playbills, sheet music, motion picture stills, theater posters, cigarette cards, greeting cards, contemporary newspaper clippings and magazine articles form important parts of our libraries. In addition, we have collected items such as Toby jugs, plates, figurines, phonograph records, and DVDs.

A Collecting Context

Spanning three generations of book collectors – and a developing fourth – we hold strong views on how to appreciate authors and their works. Bruce and I believe that book collecting as a hobby can be enhanced, if time and money permit, by a "hands on" approach to the life and times of each author collected. For example: the enjoyment of reading Mark Twain is greatly increased if one can spend a day in Hannibal, Missouri visiting his boyhood home (now a Twain museum), walking up the hill to the Widow Douglas's house, exploring Injun Joe's cave, and having a picnic lunch on the banks of the Mississippi where Tom, Huck and Jim set sail on their raft.

We have visited many such locales, such as: Sir Walter Scott's Abbotsford; Burns's Ayrshire Cottage; and the Lake District, home to Wordsworth, Coleridge and Southey. Farther afield, we have stood on the hill above Istanbul overlooking the Bosporus, where Pierre Loti is said to have been inspired to write his first book, *Aziyadé*, which was written in 1876 and relates his experiences in Constantinople. Sidney Lanier's poetry took on special significance with a visit to the grassy knoll overlooking the locale in Glynn County, Georgia where Lanier wrote his most famous poem, "The Marshes of Glynn."

For Dickens collectors, London and its environs are fascinating, since they are filled with streets, buildings and neighborhoods that figure in Dickens's life and writing. The city of Rochester, just east of London, is the Cloisterham of Edwin Drood. The Dickens House Museum in Doughty Street is a perennial favorite of ours when visiting London. Visits to Dickens's boyhood home in Portsea and his last home at Gad's Hill Place help one understand the life experiences of this famous author and Victorian celebrity.

We continue to search for Dickens material. On a recent trip to London, Bruce acquired for me an annotated Victorian album containing photographs of Dickens and his family, and compiled by the nephew of one of Dickens's sisters-in-law. Fifty years after purchasing *The Mystery of Edwin Drood* in parts, I have recently purchased the sheet music for Claude Debussy's *Hommage à S. Pickwick Esq. P.P.M.P.C., pour le piano.*

ACKNOWLEDGMENTS

Edgar Johnson's biography, *Charles Dickens: His Tragedy and Triumph* (New York: Simon and Schuster, 1952) was a valuable resource for details regarding Dickens's life and career. Ada Nisbet's book, *Dickens and Ellen Ternan* (Berkeley: University of California Press, 1952) has important information concerning the Dickens-Ternan relationship. *The Dickens Circle*, by J. W. T. Ley (New York: E. P. Dutton and Company, 1919) contains much useful information regarding Dickens's friends and associates. Edgar Brown's *Phiz and Dickens* (London: James Nisbet and Co., Limited, 1913) was useful in explaining the relationship between Dickens and Hablot K. Browne ("Phiz").

Mr. Florian Schweizer of the Dickens House Museum, Doughty Street, London was of great help in making available to us material from the museum's archives and in providing a copy of the photograph of Ellen Ternan. The Manchester Library and Information Service: Manchester Arts Library in Manchester, England provided a copy of the playbill for *The Frozen Deep*, which is reproduced with their kind permission.

We would also like to express our gratitude to the following individuals for their important contributions: Mr. Eric Holzenberg, Mr. Fernando Peña, Ms. Mary Young, Mr. George Ong, Ms. Megan Smith, and Mr. Arthur Schwarz, all with The Grolier Club of New York; Mr. Louis Lippo, Principal of the John M. Patterson School in Philadelphia; Ms. Brenda Galloway-Wright, Temple University Libraries, Urban Archives; and Mr. David Mohr, French language translator. We thank Mr. Fernando Guzman, who helped publicize our web site; Mr. Frank Sypher, who assisted in editing our work; Mr. Jerry Kelly, who designed our book; and Mr. Evan Crawford who assisted in proofreading.

We would also like to express our thanks to Mary and Helene Crawford for their advice, encouragement and support.

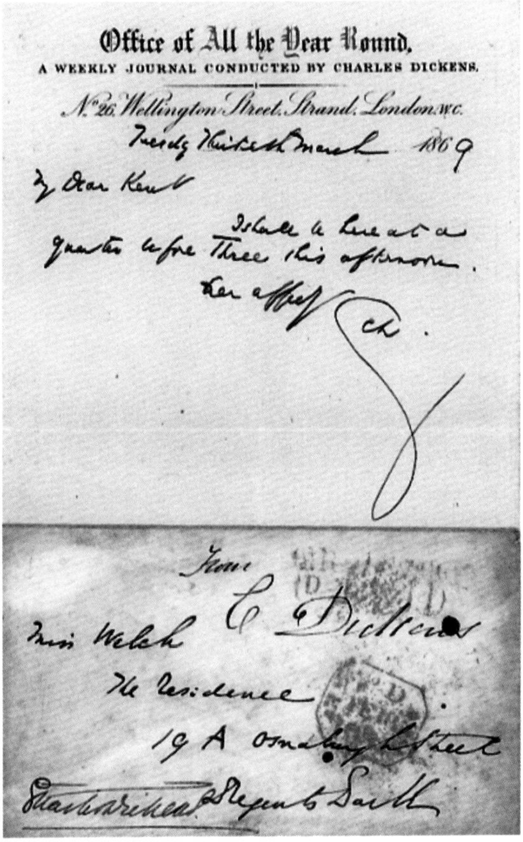

Office of All the Year Round.

A WEEKLY JOURNAL CONDUCTED BY CHARLES DICKENS.

No. 26. Wellington Street, Strand, London. W.C.

Tuesday Thirtieth March 1869

My Dear Kent

I shall be here at a quarter before Three this afternoon.

Ever affecly

CD.

From C Dickens

Miss Welch

The Residence

19 A Osnaburgh Street

Regents Park

NO. 2

CATALOGUE OF THE EXHIBITION

1] Charles Dickens. Undated reproduction of a photograph taken by C. Watkins, 1861.

Dickens, author of twenty-eight books, eight plays and operettas, as well as a contributor of scores of articles to periodicals and newspapers, was a prolific writer. This, together with his performances as an actor and his reading tours in England and America, not only enhanced his tremendous popularity, but enabled him to amass an estate of over one hundred thousand pounds, a considerable sum in 1870. Dickens's popularity continues today with dramatizations of his work on the stage, in films, television and musicals; the hit film *Oliver!* won an Academy Award, and at Christmas dramatic versions of *A Christmas Carol* are staged in school auditoriums and on television. Dickensian words are recognized in Webster's dictionary: "Scrooge" for miser; "Micawberish" for one who is improvident but who lives in expectation of an upturn in his fortunes, and "Pecksniffian" for sanctimonious hypocrisy. A lasting legacy.

2] Charles Dickens. Autograph note initialed "CD," Tuesday, March 13, 1869, to "My Dear Kent," on stationery headed "Office of All the Year Round" with a franked envelope signed by Dickens to a Miss Welch.

From being employed as a child filling bottles in a blacking (i.e., shoe polish) warehouse, to struggling young court reporter, to world-acclaimed novelist, Dickens's life was a rags-to-riches story. At age 25, after the tremendous success of *Pickwick Papers,* Dickens at times lived his life with a flourish, flamboyance and occasional bravado reminiscent of the characteristic flourish of his signature, exhibited here.

3] Prospectus for *The First Editions of the Writings of Charles Dickens and Their Values: A Bibliography,* by John C. Eckel. London: Chapman and Hall, Ltd., undated but circa 1913.

Five leaves in the Patterson archive (ten pages) comprise material related to the publication of Eckel's *Bibliography.* This item is a four-page pamphlet, and is a prospectus announcing the publication of the *Bibliography,* and giving details about it.

[25]

A DICKENS BIBLIOGRAPHY

THE FIRST EDITIONS OF THE WRITINGS OF CHARLES DICKENS
AND THEIR VALUES

A BIBLIOGRAPHY

By JOHN C. ECKEL

With a Portrait of Dickens, and 36 illustrations and fac-similes

Ordinary Edition Demy 8vo limited to 750 copies, 12s. 6d. net.

Large Paper Edition, Printed on fine deckle edge paper, limited to 250 copies, 25s. net.

T O produce a Dickens Bibliography which, by the wideness of its scope and definiteness of its treatment, should appeal to all interested in the subject, has been the purpose of Mr. John C. Eckel, the compiler of this work. Previous bibliographies have omitted any intelligent attempt at collation, so that there is no

NEW DICKENS BIBLIOGRAPHY.—Nearly half a century after the novelist's death, with all the accumulated wealth of biography, bibliography, essay, lecture, catalogue and exhibition to fall back on, it should be possible to compile a bibliography that may be considered final. Has Mr. John C. Eckel, in his *The First Editions of the Writings of Charles Dickens and their values* succeeded in doing so? Of course, in one sense, the answer must be "No," because Mr. Eckel has not attempted a complete bibliography—in fact, it is doubtful whether such a thing would be either possible or desirable. It is the first edition of a book that has the real interest for the collector, and probably always will have. Later editions may have an interest and value of their own, but the collector will never prize them as he will the *editio princeps*. Mr. Eckel was wise, therefore, in confining his attention to "first editions," and, so far as we can judge, he has done his work well, and provided the collector with a reference book that surpasses all previous attempts. The work forms a handsome 8vo volume of 374 pages, printed on thick antique paper, with a portrait of Dickens, and 36 illustrations and facsimiles. The publishers (Chapman and Hall, Limited) confined the edition to 750 numbered copies, and we understand that already they are nearly all sold, so that the bibliography will soon add scarceness to its other values. The author in his preface acknowledges assistance given by at least one English bookseller, Mr. Ernest Maggs, as also Mr. B. W. Matz, of the Dickens Fellowship, but his other helpers seem to have been Americans, which points to the fact, more and more noticeable in book-collecting, that all our rarest books go to America. Among the latter is the Secretary of the Grolier Club, Mr. Walter Gilliss, but we regret to see no mention in his preface of the valuable little catalogue of the Grolier Club Exhibition of the Works of Charles Dickens, compiled by Miss Ruth S. Granniss, and issued by the Club in 1913, which we noticed in our issue of September 27th last. The statement, therefore, in the preface that "previous bibliographies have omitted any intelligent attempt at collation" requires modifying, because, whatever may be said of the other bibliographies, Miss Granniss' work can hardly be so lightly dismissed. Take for instance, the "discovery" of a fourth variant of the first edition of *The Battle of Life*. Mr.

Eckel draws particular attention to this ing it "has the supreme merit of being genuine first issue." By the courtesy of W. B. Osgood Field, the owner of one of only three copies known to exist, the author has been able to give a facsimile of this rare and hitherto unknown issue. Of the four different title-pages (1) the one discovered first issue having the word *LOVE STORY* in plain type; (2) the observably-believed first issue, having those words engraved in a simple frame; (3) containing those words in a more elaborate frame with the date (1846) omitted; (4) the complete whole imprint omitted. This "first issue" the author states, was in the Grolier Exhibition, and he quotes the descriptor from their "Catalogue." Having, then, seen Miss Granniss' catalogue, it seems as if Mr. Eckel did not modify the words after a slip, and may be rectified in another edition. We have always considered that these days of easy reproduction by graphic processes, facsimiles of title-pages, might be more freely used than have hitherto been, and we are glad that Mr. Eckel has availed himself of it. In the case of *The Life*, a clearer idea of the four issues be gathered from a glance at the facsimiles of both in colours. His plate than could be got from pages of description of which the issue, with 1844 on title brings £50, while that with 1843 brings. We have not space here to describe what is, but Mr. Eckel puts it all very clearly, with facsimiles of both in colours. His is one which no bookseller ought to be out, and we cordially recommend it. The price is 12/6 net.

The Clique Office,
February 28th, 1914.

THE FIRST EDITIONS OF THE WRITINGS OF CHARLES DICKENS AND THEIR VALUES
A BIBLIOGRAPHY

By JOHN C. ECKEL

WITH A PORTRAIT OF CHARLES DICKENS AND 36 ILLUSTRATIONS AND FAC-SIMILES

LONDON
CHAPMAN & HALL, Ltd.
1913

4] Eckel, John C. *The First Editions of the Writings of Charles Dickens and Their Values: A Bibliography.* London: Chapman & Hall, Ltd., 1913.

Number 99 of an edition of 250 on large paper, signed by Eckel and by the Managing Director of Chapman and Hall. Judge Patterson intended to extra-illustrate this *Bibliography* with material on view at the present Grolier Club exhibition.

5] Clipped newspaper article excerpted from *The Clique Office,* February 28, 1914.

A mixed but generally favorable review of Eckel's *Bibliography.* The article mentions the Grolier Club, some of its members, and the Dickens exhibition mounted by the Club in 1913.

6] B. W. Matz. Undated reproduction of a photograph.

Matz, a Dickens scholar, edited the National Edition of the works of Charles Dickens, published in London from 1906 to 1908.

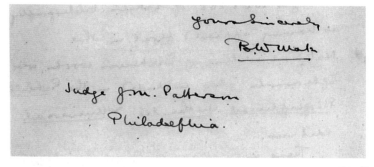

NO. 7

7] B. W. Matz. Autograph letter signed, 12 November 1914, to Judge J. M. Patterson, on stationery of *The Dickensian.*

Patterson obviously had written to Matz regarding the articles on pages 202 and 203 of Eckel's *Bibliography,* and presumably in connection with compiling this archive of extra-illustration material. In this two-page letter, Matz states that Dickens collaborated with others on articles in *Household Words.* Matz also writes, with reference to these articles, that they "would make another volume in themselves."

8] John C. Eckel. Autograph letter signed, Jan 22, 1913, to "My Dear Mr. Matz," on stationery of *The North American.*

An important letter, in which Eckel formally introduces Judge John Patterson to B. W. Matz. He says of Patterson: "Aside from being a close personal friend he has been president of our Fellowship two terms and has just been reelected for a third term. In a business way he is the assistant district attorney of Philadelphia and in addition a fine fellow. I gladly commend him to your mercies." The letter continues with Eckel's discussion of proper handling of some illustration blocks and proofs for *A Christmas Carol,* which Patterson will carry with him. The letter implies that Eckel and Matz are collaborating on a book about Dickens, soon to be in the press.

NO. 8

NO. 9   NO. 10

9] T. W. Tyrell. Autograph letter signed, 14 November 1914, to "Dear Matz."

The letter reads: "Enclosed is the portrait for which you ask. I had forgotten that I am mentioned in Mr. Eckel's bibliography, and not seeing my name in the index, had some difficulty in finding the reference." One can surmise, based on the content of this letter, that Matz collaborated with John Patterson in the latter's efforts to extra-illustrate the Eckel *Bibliography.*

10] T. W. Tyrell. Undated reproduction of a photograph.

Tyrell supplied the photographs for *Gone Astray,* the booklet written by Dickens and published by Chapman and Hall in 1912.

11] Benj. Maggs; C. Albert Maggs; and Ernest Maggs. Autograph letter signed, 29 September 1914, to "His Honor Judge J. M. Patterson," on Maggs Bros. stationery.

A fine, interesting two-page letter with Dickensian references. The three Maggs brothers express their enjoyment in discussing matters related to

NO. 11

Charles Dickens, and in their association with Patterson: "This summer was the first occasion on which we had the pleasure, Sir, of your personal acquaintance, may it not be the last, or, as Sam Weller has aptly put it, 'Wery glad to see you, indeed, and hope our acquaintance may be a long'un, as the gen'l'm'n said to the fi'pun'note' (Pickwick Papers)." Maggs Brothers published a catalogue in 1913 listing a number of the reading editions which Eckel includes in his chapter in the *Bibliography* entitled "Miscellaneous and Unclassified."

12] a. [Illustration] "Election at Eatanswill" from Part Five of *Pickwick Papers*. London: Chapman and Hall, 1836.

According to Eckel, the first-issue Phiz plate shows the Beadle's legs as straight. *Pickwick Papers*, published in serial parts beginning in 1836, was Dickens's first major novel, and lifted him to fame. The character Sam Weller, when he appeared in an early number, caught the public's attention, and sales of monthly numbers soared. To keep up with demand, publishers Chapman and Hall printed numbers with re-engraved plates, which showed minor variations from the originals.

NO. 12A

NO. 12B

NO. 12E

NO. 12F

b. [Illustration] "Election at Eatanswill" from Part Five of *Pickwick Papers*. London: Chapman and Hall, 1836–37.

A later-issue Phiz plate shows the Beadle's legs as bow-legged.

c. [Illustration] "Conviviality at Bob Sawyer's" from Part Fourteen of *Pickwick Papers*. London: Chapman and Hall, 1836.

According to Eckel, the first-state plate has the books on the top shelf of the bookcase lying down.

d. [Illustration] "Conviviality at Bob Sawyer's" from Part Fourteen of *Pickwick Papers*. London: Chapman and Hall, 1836–37.

A later-state plate has the books on the top shelf standing upright.

e. [Illustration] "Mrs. Bardell Encounters Mr. Pickwick in Prison" from Part Sixteen of *Pickwick Papers*. London: Chapman and Hall, 1836.

According to Eckel, the first-state plate has a railing on the steps and a cockade in Sam Weller's hat.

f. [Illustration] "Mrs. Bardell Encounters Mr. Pickwick in Prison" from Part Sixteen of *Pickwick Papers*. London: Chapman and Hall, 1836–37.

A later-state plate has no railing on the steps and no cockade in Sam Weller's hat.

g. [Illustration] "Mary and the Fat Boy" from Parts Nineteen and Twenty of *Pickwick Papers*. London: Chapman and Hall, 1836.

According to Eckel, the first-state plate shows the knife in the boy's hand pointing down.

h. [Illustration] "Mary and the Fat Boy" from Parts Nineteen and Twenty of *Pickwick Papers*. London: Chapman and Hall, 1836–37.

A later-state plate shows the knife in the boy's hand pointing up.

13] [Illustration] The "Fireside" plate from *Oliver Twist*. London: Richard Bentley, 1838.

According to Eckel, the presence of this plate indicates a first issue of the first edition. The plate was cancelled in later issues.

"PHIZ."

NO. 13   NO. 14

14] Hablot K. Browne ("Phiz"). Undated reproduction of a drawn portrait.

"Phiz" drew a sketch of Dickens for the *Extraordinary Gazette*. The *Gazette* parodied a typical "Royal Speech" and, using bombastic and ponderous language, announced the coming of *Oliver Twist* as a serial in *Bentley's Miscellany*.

15] Charles Dickens. *Extraordinary Gazette*. London: Richard Bentley, 1837.

The pamphlet announces the appearance in *Bentley's Miscellany* of *Oliver Twist*. The "Phiz" illustration on page one of the pamphlet shows Dickens making a speech as "His Mightiness."

16] Page two of the *Extraordinary Gazette* (see Item 15).

Two leaves (four pages) in the Patterson archive comprise this pamphlet, inserted in *Bentley's Miscellany*. *Oliver Twist* is not referred to in the "Speech," as Dickens cleverly mentions it only as the "punch line" in a "note of the reporter" at the end of the pamphlet. In this "note" the "reporter" writes: "His Mightiness incorporated with his speech on gen-

Extraordinary Gazette.

SPEECH OF HIS MIGHTINESS

ON OPENING THE SECOND NUMBER

OF

BENTLEY'S MISCELLANY,

EDITED BY "BOZ."

On Wednesday, the first of February, "the House" (of Bentley) met for the despatch of business, in pursuance of the Proclamation inserted by authority in all the Morning, Evening, and Weekly Papers, appointing that day for the publication of the Second Number of the Miscellany, edited by "Boz."

NO. 15

---

2   BENTLEY'S MISCELLANY.

His Mightiness the Editor, in his progress to New Burlington-street, received with the utmost affability the numerous petitions of the crossing-sweepers; and was, repeatedly and loudly hailed by the cabmen on the different stands in the line of road through which he passed. His Mightiness appeared in the highest possible spirits; and immediately after his arrival at the House, delivered himself of the following most gracious speech:

"My Lords, Ladies, and Gentlemen:

"In calling upon you to deliberate on the various important matters which I have now to submit to your consideration, I rely with entire confidence on that spirit of good-will and kindness of which I have more than once taken occasion to express my sense; and which I am but too happy to acknowledge again.

"It has been the constant aim of my policy to preserve peace in your minds, and promote merriment in your hearts; to set before you, the scenes and characters of real life in all their endless diversity; occasionally (I hope) to instruct, always to amuse, and never to offend. I trust I may refer you to my Pickwick an measures, already taken and still in progress, in confirmation of this assurance.

"In further proof of my sincere anxiety for the amusement and light-heartedness of the community, let me direct your particular attention to the volume I now lay before you, which contains no fewer than twenty-one reports, of greater or less extent, from most eminent, active, and intelligent commissioners. I cannot but anticipate that when you shall have given an attentive perusal to this general report on Periodical Literature, you will be seized with an eager and becoming desire to possess yourselves of all the succeeding numbers,—a desire on which too much praise and encouragement can never be bestowed.

"Gentlemen of the Reviews:

"I have directed the earliest copies of every monthly number to be laid before you. They shall be framed

NO. 16

BENTLEY'S MISCELLANY.   3

with the strictest regard to the taste and wishes of the people; and I am confident that I may rely on your zealous and impartial co-operation in the public service.

"The accounts and estimates of the first number have been made out; and I am happy to inform you that the state of the revenue as compared with the expenditure (great as the latter has been, and must necessarily continue to be) is most satisfactory; in fact, that a surplus of considerable extent has been already realised. It affords me much pleasure to reflect that not the smallest difficulty will arise, in the appropriation of it.

"My Lords, Ladies, and Gentlemen:

"I continue to receive from Foreign Powers, undeniable assurances of their disinterested regard and esteem. The free and independent States of America have done me the honour to reprint my Sketches, gratuitously; and to circulate them throughout the Possessions of the British Crown in India, without charging me anything at all. I think I shall recognize Don Carlos if I ever meet him in the street; and I am sure I shall at once know the King of the French, for I have seen him before.

"I deeply lament the ferment and agitation of the public mind in Ireland, which was occasioned by the inadequate supply of the first number of this Miscellany. I deplore the outrages which were committed by an irritated and disappointed populace on the shop of the agent; and the violent threats which were directed against him, personally, on his stating his inability to comply with their exorbitant demands. I derive great satisfaction from reflecting that the promptest and most vigorous measures were instantaneously taken to repress the tumult. A large detachment of Miscellanies was levied and shipped with all possible despatch; and I have it in my power to state, that, although the excitement has not yet wholly subsided, it has been, by these means, materially allayed. I have every reason to hope that the arrangements since made with my agent in the Port of Dublin, render any recurrence of the disturbances extremely

NO. 17

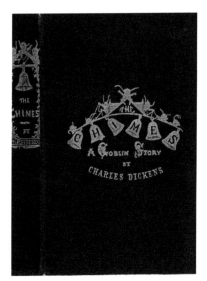

NO. 19

eral topics some especial reference to one Oliver Twist, not directly understanding the illusion, we have abstained from giving it."

17] Page three of the *Extraordinary Gazette* (see Item 15).

18] [Playbill] Theatre Royal, Tavistock House [London]: January 8, 1855.

Charles Dickens loved Christmas, and celebrated the season in several ways: through his numerous Christmas stories of course, but also through personal and family endeavors. It would seem that Dickens viewed Christmas not so much as a religious holiday, but as a season of good food and drink, and a time for the gathering of family and friends for entertainment and hijinks. Dickens loved children, and during each Christmas season, held children's parties at which he performed conjuring tricks, sang comic songs, and presided at a festive dinner followed by dancing. He also produced Twelfth Night plays, the cast consisting of the children, adult friends, and members of his family. Typical of these Twelfth Night performances is the playbill exhibited here. For this performance on January 8, 1855, the nursery at Tavistock House was converted to a theater with a stage. Planché's farce *Fortunio and His Seven Gifted Servants* was produced. The cast included Wilkie Collins as Wilkini Collini, Mark Lemon as Strongback, and Dickens in two roles: as Mr. Passe, and as Mr. Measley Servile. Among the children, Mr. Ainger is Alfred Ainger, a little friend of the Dickens children. Henry Dickens is Mr. H, and Edward Dickens, not yet three, plays Mr. Plornishmaroontigoonter.

19] Original crimson front cloth cover and backstrip, from *The Chimes* by Charles Dickens. London: Chapman and Hall, 1845.

The first issue of the first edition (as here) has a bright crimson cover with gilt stamps on the side and backstrip. In this Christmas book, Dickens continued with his social-protest theme of "rich vs. poor"; some of the characters (e.g., Alderman Bowley and Sir Joseph) represent the rich establishment, while others (e.g., Trotty Veck and Meg) represent the poor.

20] a. [Illustrations] The frontispiece and title page from *The Chimes*. London: Chapman and Hall, 1845.

Altogether in the first edition of Dickens's *The Chimes*, there are thirteen illustrations, including these two by Daniel Maclise. Of the other eleven illustrations, John Leech did five, Clarkson Stanfield two, and Richard Doyle, four.

b. [Illustration] The Daniel Maclise drawing, undated, published by C. H. Jeens, of Dickens reading in December 1844 from *The Chimes*, to a circle of his friends, including W. J. Fox, John Forster, and others.

c. [Illustrations] Woodcut for "First Quarter," chapter heading of *The Chimes*.

Mounted adjacent on the same sheet is the illustration of Toby ("Trotty") Veck, from the first edition of *The Chimes*.

d. [Illustrations] Trotty Veck, Alderman Cute, and the "Red-faced Gentleman" from the first edition of *The Chimes*.

Mounted adjacent on the same sheet is a woodcut for the chapter entitled "The Second Quarter," in *The Chimes*.

e. [Illustrations] Trotty Veck, Mr. Fish, Sir Joseph Bowley, and Lady Bowley from the first edition of *The Chimes*.

This illustration also shows two views of Sir Joseph's porter. Mounted adjacent on the same sheet is the illustration of Trotty Veck at the church.

f. [Illustrations] Woodcut for "Third Quarter," chapter heading of *The Chimes*.

This illustration shows Trotty Veck, and the Goblins and Elves swarming from the church bells. Mounted adjacent on the same sheet, also from the first edition of *The Chimes*, is the illustration of Will Fern and the cottage, with a lady sketching them.

g. [Illustrations] Margaret (Meg) at her needlework, and in the foreground, Richard returning to the cottage from the first edition of *The Chimes*.

Mounted adjacent on the same sheet is a woodcut for "Fourth Quarter," chapter heading of *The Chimes*, showing the phantoms as ghostly figures emerging from the Bells.

Theatre Royal, Tavistock House.

RE-ENGAGEMENT OF THAT IRRESISTIBLE COMEDIAN, MR. AINGER!

RE-APPEARANCE OF MR. H. WHO CREATED SO POWERFUL AN IMPRESSION LAST YEAR!

RETURN OF MR. CHARLES DICKENS, JUNIOR, FROM HIS GERMAN ENGAGEMENTS!

ENGAGEMENT OF MISS KATE, WHO DECLINED THE MUNIFICENT OFFERS OF THE MANAGEMENT LAST SEASON!

MR. PASSÉ, MR. MUDPERIOD, MR. MEASLEY SERVILE, AND MR. WILKINI COLLINI!

FIRST APPEARANCE ON ANY STAGE OF MR. PLORNISHMAROONTIGOONTER!

(Who has been kept out of bed at a vast expence.)

ON MONDAY EVENING, JANUARY 8TH, 1855,

WILL BE PRESENTED

MR. PLANCHÉ'S FAIRY EXTRAVAGANZA, IN TWO ACTS, WITH ALTERATIONS BY THE DRAMATIC POET OF THIS ESTABLISHMENT, CALLED

FORTUNIO,

AND HIS SEVEN GIFTED SERVANTS

DRAMATIS PERSONÆ.

THE PROCLAMATION.

BARON DUNOVER (*a Nobleman in Difficulties*)	MR. PASSE.
HONORABLE MISS PERTINA (*his eldest Daughter*)	MISS KATE.
HONORABLE MISS FLIRTINA (*his second Daughter*)	MISS LALLY.
HONORABLE MISS MYRTINA (*his youngest Daughter, assuming the name and titles of* FORTUNIO)	} MR. H.
HERALD OF KING ALFOURITE	MR. WALTER.
THE FAIRY QUEEN	MISS BETTY LEMON.
PAGE	MR. SYDNEY SMITH.
STANDARD-BEARERS	MISS NELLY and MR. DAVID.
COMRADE (*a Learned Horse*)	MR. CUMUP.

THE SEVEN GIFTED SERVANTS.

STRONGBACK, with the gift of Strength	MR. MARK LEMON, JUN.
LIGHTFOOT, with the gift of Swiftness	MR. PLORNISHMAROONTIGOONTER.
MARKSMAN, with the gift of Far-Sight	MR. FRANK.
FINE-EAR, with the gift of Quick Hearing	MR. HARRY.
BOISTERER, with the gift of Mighty Lungs	MR. ALLY.
GORMAND, with the gift of Appetite	MR. WILKINI COLLINI.
TIPPLER, with the gift of Thirst	MR. MARKHAM NESFIELD.

THE PRESENTATION.

KING ALFOURITE	MR. CHARLES DICKENS, JUN.
PRINCESS VINDICTA (*his Half-sister*)	MISS DICKENS.
FLORIDA (*her Lady in Waiting*)	MISS EDITH BRADBURY.
THE DRAGON	MR. MUDPERIOD.

THE EMBASSY.

THE EMPEROR MATAPA (*Cousin to the Great Bear*)	MR. AINGER.
PRINCESS VOLANTE (*his Daughter, a high-mettled Racer*)	MISS BERTHA STONE.
THE GRAND CHAMBERLAIN	MR. EDWARD HOGARTH.
THE CAPTAIN OF THE GUARD	MR. MARCUS.
THE EXPECTANT COUSIN OF THE NOBILITY IN GENERAL	MR. MEASLEY SERVILE.

MISS HOGARTH WILL PRESIDE AT THE PIANO FORTE.

MESSRS. NATHAN, *of Titchbourne Street, are the Costumiers ;* MR. WILSON, *of the Strand, is the Perruquier ; and* MR. THOMAS IRELAND, *of the Adelphi Theatre, is the Maker of the Properties to this vast Establishment.*

GOD SAVE THE QUEEN!

NO. 20A

NO. 20B

h. [Illustration] Trotty Veck leading Mrs. Chickenstalker in the dance with Meg and Richard as "second couple," from the first edition of *The Chimes*.

21] [Illustrations] Frontispiece and title page, designed by Daniel Maclise, for *The Battle of Life*. London: Bradbury and Evans, 1846.

This fourth variant title page to the first edition is of great bibliographic interest to collectors. According to Eckel, the Grolier Club figures importantly in the discovery of previously unknown variants of the first edition of *The Battle of Life*. First, William B. Osgood Field, a member of the Grolier, was the owner of the second variant, of which there were only three known copies, one of which he made available to Eckel and to the Grolier Club's *Exhibition of the Works of Charles Dickens*, held January 28 to March 8, 1913. Second, the Grolier exhibition also included a copy of the first variant, previously unknown and of great rarity. All four variants of *The Battle of Life* title page were illustrated in the 1913 catalogue issued by the Club for that exhibition. This illustration was reproduced by Eckel in his *Bibliography*, as a foldout after page 128.

NO. 21

22] Original front cover for *Dombey and Son. Full-length Portraits.* London: Chapman and Hall, 1848.

In 1848, Hablot K. Browne ("Phiz") drew two series of extra-illustrations for *Dombey.* These extra-illustrations were etched by Browne and R. Young. The first series of plates depicts Edith, Florence, Alice, and Little Paul. The second series depicts Dombey and Carker, Miss Tox, Mrs. Skewton, Mrs. Pipchin, Old Sol and Captain Cuttle, Major Bagstock, Miss Nipper, and Polly. Both series of extra-illustrations were published by Chapman and Hall with the sanction of Dickens. This item is the original front cover from the second series of plates.

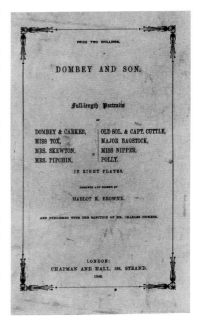

23] a. [Illustration] "Dombey and Carker," the first plate in the second series of extra-illustrations for *Dombey and Son,* drawn by Hablot K. Browne.

b. [Illustration] "Miss Tox," the second plate in the second series of extra-illustrations for *Dombey and Son,* drawn by Hablot K. Browne.

c. [Illustration] "Mrs. Skewton," the third plate in the second series of extra-illustrations for *Dombey and Son,* drawn by Hablot K. Browne.

d. [Illustration] "Mrs. Pipchin," the fourth plate in the second series of extra-illustrations for *Dombey and Son,* drawn by Hablot K. Browne.

e. [Illustration] "Old Sol and Captain Cuttle," the fifth plate in

the second series of extra-illustrations for *Dombey and Son,*
drawn by Hablot K. Browne.

f. [Illustration] "Major Bagstock," the sixth plate in the second

NO. 23A

NO. 23B

NO. 23G

NO. 23H

series of extra-illustrations for *Dombey and Son,* drawn by Hablot K. Browne.

g. [Illustration] "Miss Nipper," the seventh plate in the second series of extra-illustrations for *Dombey and Son,* drawn by Hablot K. Browne.

h. [Illustration] "Polly," the eighth and last plate in the second series of extra-illustrations for *Dombey and Son,* drawn by Hablot K. Browne.

24] Original green front wrapper from Part II of *The Mystery of Edwin Drood.* London: Chapman & Hall, 1870.

This cover was designed by Charles A. Collins, who was a brother of Wilkie Collins, and the husband of Charles Dickens's daughter, Kate. Except for the cover, the illustrations to *Drood* were done by Luke Fildes. In Dickens's decision to write a mystery, he was probably influenced by the popularity of mystery novels written by his friend, Wilkie Collins, notably, *The Moonstone* and *The Woman in White.* It is ironic that *The Mystery of Edwin Drood,* unfinished because of Dickens's

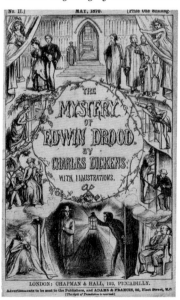

death, should have engendered more controversy than any of his more important works. The identity of the murderer of Edwin Drood was unknown to the publishers, Chapman & Hall, who in a page appended to the last number, stated: "All that was left in manuscript of *Edwin Drood* is contained in the number now published – the sixth . . . the only notes in reference to the story that have since been found concern that portion of it exclusively, which is treated in the earlier Numbers. Beyond the clues therein afforded to its conduct or catastrophe, nothing whatever remains. . . . " However, John Forster, close friend and confidant of Dickens, said that John Jasper was the murderer. Furthermore, Charles Dickens, Jr. said that his father told him that Jasper would be disclosed as the killer. Charles Collins, the designer of the cover, said that Dickens insisted that Jasper, shown in the upper right-hand corner of the cover, looking thoughtfully at Edwin and Rosa, wear a long scarf with which he would strangle Edwin. Nevertheless, over the years and despite this contemporary evidence, scores of books have been published offering solutions to the mystery and conclusions to the novel. These include *The Mystery of Edwin Drood Complete,* in which the novel was purportedly finished by Dickens, from the afterworld, through a spiritualist medium. The "medium" went on to state that the next book to be published by Dickens from the spirit world would be *The Life and Adventures of Bookley Wickleheap.* Thankfully, this was never published. Even R. Austin Freeman, creator of the *Dr. Thorndyke Mysteries,* had a hand at *Edwin Drood,* writing a spoof, *The Mystery of Angelina Frood.* Of course, *The Trial of John Jasper,* published by Judge John Patterson, is of this genre of sequels.

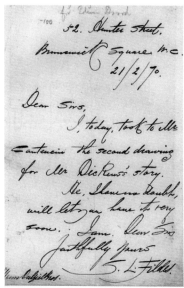

NO. 25   NO. 26

25] Luke Fildes, A.R.A. Undated reproduction of a drawn portrait.

Fildes was the illustrator of *Edwin Drood*. While he was acquainted with Dickens for only the few months immediately prior to Dickens's death in June 1870, Fildes had a great admiration for the novelist. Shortly after Dickens's death, Fildes painted *The Empty Chair*, showing Dickens's study at Gad's Hill as Dickens left it.

26] Luke Fildes, A.R.A. Autograph letter signed, February 21, 1870 from Brunswick Square, to "Dear Sirs."

This letter discusses in part the "second drawing for Mr. Dickens's story" (i.e. *The Mystery of Edwin Drood*).

Items 27–34, related to *The Strange Gentleman* and *The Village Coquettes*, illustrate Dickens's lifelong interest in acting and the stage. His work as a playwright began with these two plays.

27] J. P. Harley. Undated reproduction of a photograph.

The comedian Harley is pictured here in the leading role from *The Strange Gentleman*, a play by Dickens published in 1837. "The Great Winglebury Duel" in *Sketches by Boz* was the basis of this farce. The first performance of *The Strange Gentleman* was given on September 29, 1836. Harley played the title role for sixty nights. Another in the cast was Madame Sala, the mother of George Augustus Sala.

28] [Playbill] Theatre-Royal, Liverpool: September 5, 1838.

This playbill announces the performances of *Wild Oats, The Strange Gentleman,* and *Loan of a Lover*. Harley acts here in the lead role as "The Strange Gentleman."

29] J. P. Harley. Autograph letter signed, 15 January 1857, to "My Dear Sir" [H. Watkins, Esq.].

Harley played the leading role in Dickens's play *The Strange Gentleman*. A jocular two-page letter to a friend, albeit on mourning stationery, with reference to a well-known English comic song, "The Old English Gentleman."

30] John Braham. Undated engraving after H. Adlard.

Braham, shown here as he appeared in 1800 was Manager of the New

St. James Theater. He had produced *The Strange Gentleman*, and in 1836 he accepted a comic opera, written by Charles Dickens and John Hullah, entitled *The Village Coquettes*. According to Eckel, *The Village Coquettes* had its first presentation on December 6, 1836 with Braham in the cast. This play was dedicated to J. P. Harley, who also took part in

NO. 27

CHARLES DICKENS

THEATRE-ROYAL, LIVERPOOL,

Second Week of

Mr. HARLEY.

Third appearance of

Mr. and Mrs. KEELEY,

Who are engaged for TEN NIGHTS.

Third Week of

Mr. F. VINING.

This present WEDNESDAY, Sept. 5, 1838,

Will be performed O'Keefe's celebrated Comedy, called

WILD OATS.

Ephraim Smooth..Mr. HARLEY
Rover..Mr. F. VINING
Sim..Mr. KEELEY

Sir George Thunder............ Mr. GRANBY | Landlord............Mr. CUNNINGHAM
Harry Thunder............Mr. W. H. BLAND | Waiter............Mr. ENGLAND
Banks............Mr. GRAY | Zachariah............Mr. F. LLOYDS
Farmer Gammon............Mr. WEBSTER |
John Dory............Mr. CHAPLIN | Lady Amaranth............Miss FAUCIT
Lamp............Mr. BENWELL | Amelia............Miss CLEAVER
Trap............Mr. J. RIDGWAY | Servants............Mesds. GRANBY, BENWELL,
Midge............Mr. T. RIDGWAY | COOMBE, WEBSTER, Miss WEBSTER, and
Twitch............Mr. JONAS | Miss GRANBY
Jane............Mrs. KEELEY,

In which character she will introduce a Song written by the late J. Pocock, Esq., called

" *To the Fields I carry my milking can* "

Previous to the Play,

Overture—"M.S."—De Val.

After which will be produced, for the first time here, a new Farce, written by " Hoz," called the

STRANGE GENTLEMAN.

The Strange Gentleman......(just arrived at the St. James's Arms)......Mr. HARLEY,

As originally performed by him in London.

Mr. Owen Overton { Mayor of a small town on the road to Gretna, and useful { Mr. GRANBY
at the St. James's Arms,

John Johnson.........(Detained at the St. James's Arms)......Mr. J. RIDGWAY
Charles Tomkins........(Incognito at the St. James's Arms)......Mr. W. H. BLAND
Tom Sparks..........(a one-eyed " Boots," at the St. James's Arms)......Mr. BAKER
John.....{ ...Mr. ENGLAND
Joe.. ...{ Waiters at the St. James's Arms, { ...Mr. CUNNINGHAM
Will..... { ...Mr. T. RIDGWAY
Julia Dobbs...(Looking for a Husband at the St. James's Arms)......Mrs. GRANBY
Fanny Wilson.........(with an Appointment at the St. James's Arms)......Miss CLEAVER
Mary Wilson.............(her Sister, awkwardly situated at the St. James's Arms).........Miss FAUCIT
Mrs. Noakes.........(the Landlady at the St. James's Arms)......Mrs. EDWARDS
Chambermaid......(at the St. James's Arms).......Mrs E. BENWELL

Previous to the Afterpiece,

Overture—Schneider

To conclude with the Drama, in one act, of a

LOAN OF A LOVER.

Peter Spyk............Mr. KEELEY
Captain Amersfort............ Mr. W. HOWARD | Swyzel............Mr. GRANBY
Delve............Mr. JONAS | Ernestine Rosendaal............Miss CLEAVER
Gertrude............Mrs. KEELEY

Incidental to the Piece the following Songs, &c.:—
Duet—"To-morrow will be market day,"............By Mr. and Mrs KEELEY
Song—" I don't think I'm ugly."............By Mrs. KEELEY
Song—" I've no money, so you see,"............By Mrs. KEELEY
Duet—" But that is rather doubtful,"............By Mr. GRANBY and Mrs. KEELEY
Duet—" I trust to my fate,"............By Mr. and Mrs. KEELEY

LOWER BOXES, 4s.; UPPER BOXES, 3s. 6d; PIT, 2s 6d; GALLERY, 1s.
Doors to be Opened at Half-past Six, and the Performance to commence at Seven o'Clock.
The Box-office will be open daily from Ten until Three, when Tickets and places for the Boxes may be
had of Mr. PARKER.

On THURSDAY, the new Drama of the

HOUSEKEEPER.

Sidney Maynard...Mr. F. VINING, as originally performed by him in London.
Simon Box ....Mr. KEELEY | Felicia.......Mrs. KEELEY

After which, for the second time, the new Farce of the

STRANGE GENTLEMAN.

To conclude with the Farce of

TURNING THE TABLES.

Jack Humphreys............Mr. HARLEY

On FRIDAY—Favourite Entertainments, in which Mr. HARLEY, Mr. F. VINING, Mr. KEELEY,
and Mrs. KEELEY, will perform, being for the BENEFIT OF MR. F. VINING.

NO. 28

[46]

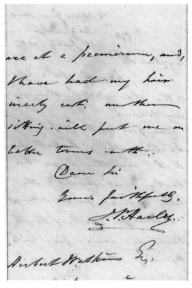

NO. 29   NO. 30

it. It is said that Harley began his stage reputation with this play. The play was published in 1836, the title reading *The Village Coquettes: A Comic Opera in Two Acts by Charles Dickens, the Music by John Hullah.*

31] John Braham. Autograph letter signed, May 26, 1832, to "Dear Sir."

The letter is written to James Wallach, the acting manager of the Drury Lane Theater. In this indignant letter, producer and actor Braham says: "No consideration will ever induce me to undergo the degradation of being dragged before an audience at one o'clock in the morning. It is as mortifying to the feelings of a performer as annoying to an audience. I therefore (seeing where you placed 'Maraniello') must decline performing on the 1st of June at Drury Lane Theatre."

32] J. M. Hullah. Autograph letter signed, June 22, 1870, to "My Dear Macmillan."

Mounted adjacent to this letter is a reproduction of a photograph of J. M. Hullah. Hullah composed the music for Dickens's comic opera, *The Village Coquettes.*

NO. 31

The Lange
Brompton
May 26th 1832

174

Dear Si

No consideration will ever induce
me to undergo the degradation of being
dragged before an audience at one o'clock
in the morning It is as mortifying to the
feelings of a Performer as annoying to an
audience — I therefore (seeing when you
placed "Masaniello") must Decline
Performing on the 1st of June at
Douglass Theatre —

I am Dear Si
Your most obt st
John Braham

June 22d 1870

174 265 11, Devonshire Place, W.

My dear Macmillan

I have received the
enclosed. Is it worth notice?

Always yours truly
John Hullah

NO. 32

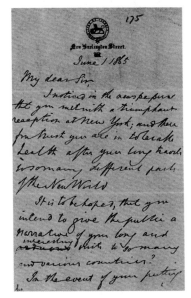

NO. 33   NO. 34

33] Richard Bentley. Undated engraving by Joseph Brown, from a
photograph by Messrs. Lock and Whitfield.

Bentley published *Bentley's Miscellany* and *The Village Coquettes,* as
well as other works by Charles Dickens.

34] Richard Bentley. Autograph letter signed, June 1, 1865, to "My
Dear Sir."

The three-page letter is written to Charles Kean, the famous actor and
son of the Shakespearean actor Edmund Kean. In this letter, Bentley
congratulates Kean on his triumphant reception in New York. He says
that he hopes Kean intends to give the public a narrative of his travels,
and that, if Kean decides to write such a work, it would be "greeted with
great welcome here." Bentley goes on to say that inasmuch as he has
already published an account of Kean's life, he expects he will be given
the opportunity to negotiate with Kean for the publication of a book of
travels, if Kean decides to write one.

35] Augustus Egg. Undated reproduction of a drawn portrait.

Dickens, along with Wilkie Collins, Mark Lemon, and others formed the Guild of Literature and Art in the 1850s. The Guild was to aid indigent artists and authors, and to provide free homes for them. As part of the Guild's activities, Dickens organized, and was the stage manager for the Company of Strolling Players. Dickens was to write a farce for the production of the company, but pressure of time prevented him from doing so and a farce constructed by Mark Lemon, editor of *Punch* and close friend of Dickens, was chosen. In the process of rehearsal, Dickens (who was to be in the cast) made so many changes that one might say the farce, *Mr. Nightingale's Diary*, is the joint effort of Dickens and Lemon. The farce was first produced on May 16, 1851. The cast included Augustus Egg (pictured here), Mark Lemon, Wilkie Collins, Dickens and others. According to Eckel, there are only three known copies of the first edition of the farce, one of which was included in the Grolier Club Dickens exhibition of 1913. The copy in that exhibition had belonged to Wilkie Collins.

36] Wilkie Collins. Autograph letter signed, July 14, 1857, to "My Dear Sir."

The four-page letter is written to the photographer Herbert Watkins,

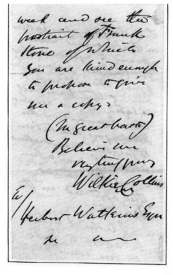

NO. 35   NO. 36

Esq. In this letter, Collins thanks Watkins for some photographs, and compliments him on their excellence. He also deplores the reproduction of a Watkins photograph that had recently appeared in *The News*. Collins, the author of many popular novels, including *The Moonstone* and *The Woman in White*, was a member (along with Dickens) of the Guild of Literature and Art, and was in the cast of the Guild's production *Mr. Nightingale's Diary*.

37] Charles Fechter. Reproduction of a portrait drawn on stone by Richard Lanel, published August 10, 1864 by J. Mitchell, Bookseller and Publisher to the Queen, and by Special Appointment to the Emperor Napoleon III.

Fechter was a noted French actor who starred in Shakespearean tragedies as well as in productions such as *Ruy Blas* and *Lady of Lyon*. In 1867 Wilkie Collins and Fechter collaborated on a stage version of *No Thoroughfare*, which had appeared as a Christmas Number in Dickens's periodical *All the Year Round*. The prologue for the stage version was written by Dickens. Fechter starred in the first performance of the play in 1867. The play achieved great popularity in England, France and America, and Dickens felt that the play would not have achieved this popularity had it not been for Fechter's guidance. In appreciation, Dickens contributed an enthusiastic article entitled "On Mr. Fechter's Acting" to the August 1869 number of the *Atlantic Monthly*. The article served to introduce Fechter to the American public.

38] Charles Fechter. Autograph letter signed, undated, to an unidentified correspondent referred to as "Charley" in the letter.

The letter (in French; here quoted in translation) opens with "By God! My very dear Charley, this time without a doubt you are crazy!" In this very emotional letter, Fechter expresses his shock and disappointment at the addressee's exposure of some indiscretions (the addressee is probably not Charles Dickens). Fechter says in part "Are these your proofs? Has Ireland gone to your head? Have a few 'Paddy' persuaded you that my affection for you has diminished?" Fechter implies that his reputation has been tarnished by the addressee's conduct in exposing a list of names that the public now associates with his theater. Fechter and

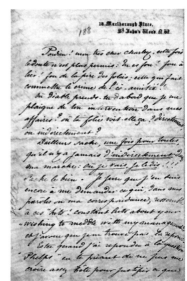

NO. 37   NO. 38

Wilkie Collins collaborated on a stage version of *No Thoroughfare*, which had appeared as a Christmas Number in Dickens's periodical *All the Year Round.*

39] Baroness Burdett Coutts. Undated reproduction of a photograph.

This item is mounted adjacent to a third-person letter from Coutts, to whom *Martin Chuzzlewit* was dedicated. The baroness had inherited immense wealth and decided that she would devote her life to helping those less fortunate. She chose the young novelist Dickens as the one to help guide her in these good works. Dickens's ability to advise the baroness resulted first-hand from his frequent walks late at night, sometimes all night, through the seamy, crime-ridden parts of London. He walked alone, or occasionally with Wilkie Collins. His celebrity enabled him to accompany the detective police in their attempts to stop or solve crimes in the London underworld. Dickens took the Baroness Coutts on a tour of the slums in the East End of London, and the baroness financed the construction of a large housing project for the poor. Dickens showed her the plight of a large number of London prostitutes, and the baroness established a home for "fallen women." These, and many other charitable endeavors, earned her a burial place in Westminster Abbey. On the personal side, she also became a close friend and confidant of Dickens. She assisted several of Dickens's sons by paying for their education. She also helped them find meaningful employment. The baroness also attempted, unsuccessfully, to reconcile Dickens and Catherine during their marital difficulties.

NO. 39

THE BARONESS BURDETT COUTTS.

NO. 40

NO. 41

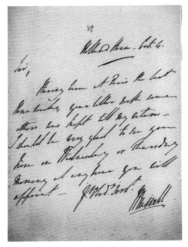

NO. 42

NO. 43

40] Richard Watson. Undated reproduction of a line drawing, from a portrait at Rockingham Castle.

David Copperfield was dedicated to Richard Watson and his wife. Watson was a member of Parliament, and Dickens shared Watson's liberal political views. They became close friends, and Dickens produced several private theatricals at Rockingham Castle.

41] Lord John Russell. Holborn: John Saunders, June 7 [n.y.]. Proof from a drawing by H. Room, after a bust by P. Hollings and engraved by W. Holl.

A Tale of Two Cities was dedicated to Lord Russell. Lord Russell was a member of Parliament, and introduced the Reform Bill, which proposed reform of the electoral system. Dickens admired Lord Russell, and was an ardent supporter of this proposal. Dickens protested vigorously when the outbreak of the Crimean War forced Lord Russell to withdraw the Bill in 1854.

42] Lord John Russell. Autograph letter signed, October 5, 1830 [on verso], to "Sir."

The letter confirms an appointment.

43] Sir James Emerson Tennent. Undated reproduction of a photograph.

Tennent was a liberal politician who shared Dickens's views on social reform. They became friends and traveled together in Italy. Dickens dedicated *Our Mutual Friend* to Tennent.

44] Francis Lord Jeffrey. Autograph letter signed, May 21 [n.y.], to Dr. S. Brown, Waddington.

Mounted adjacent to the letter is an undated reproduction of a photograph of a portrait painted by Calvin Smith of Lord Jeffrey. Lord Jeffrey was the dedicatee of *The Cricket on the Hearth*, editor of the *Edinburgh Review*, and a Scottish M.P. He was noted for writing perceptive but sometimes caustic literary reviews. He admired Dickens's *The Old Curiosity Shop*. Jeffrey pleaded with Dickens not to let Little Nell die, and upon reading in the monthly number of Little Nell's death, he broke down and cried. According to J. W. T. Ley, in his book *The Dickens Circle*, published by Dutton in 1919, Jeffrey exclaimed to a neighbor "You'll be sorry to hear that Little Nellie, Boz's Little Nellie, is dead."

45] Marcus Stone. Autograph letter signed, January 27, 1863, to "My dear Watkins," on Russell House stationery.

In this three-page letter, Stone mentions William Frith, who painted a portrait of Dickens. The letter is signed "With best wishes, yours truly." Stone illustrated *Our Mutual Friend*. Marcus Stone's father, Frank Stone, A.R.A., illustrated several books by Dickens and the two were close friends; their children played together and Marcus Stone was treated like one of the Dickens family. Upon Frank Stone's death, Dickens took Marcus under his wing and in addition to *Our Mutual Friend*, steered commissions his way, including the Library Edition of several of Dickens's works, notably *Great Expectations* and *Little Dorrit*.

46] W. J. Fox. Autograph letter initialed [June 30, 1846], to "Dearie."

The letter is mounted with a franked envelope addressed to "Miss Fox, Post Office, Ambleside." Fox was Dickens's friend, a Unitarian Preacher, and publisher of the *Daily News*. The letter (a pencil note in Patterson's hand indicates that the addressee is Fox's daughter) deals with several subjects, including activities of John Forster and Sir Robert Peel, who was instrumental in the abolition of the English corn laws, which had caused hardship for the poor. W. J. Fox, according to Dickens's biographer Edgar Johnson, was not just a friend of Dickens but also influenced him in favor of Unitarian beliefs, and thus contrary to beliefs of the Church of England, under which Dickens was raised as a child.

47] Thomas Carlyle. Autograph letter initialed, undated, to Leigh Hunt [on verso].

In the letter Carlyle complains of a headache and an inability to keep an appointment.

48] Thomas Carlyle. Undated reproduction of a line drawing by Samuel Lawrence and engraved by J. C. Armytage.

The friendship between the reclusive Scottish Puritan Thomas Carlyle and the outgoing, convivial Dickens seems an unlikely one. Carlyle,

NO. 44

NO. 45   NO. 46

[57]

writer of serious non-fiction, once referred to *Pickwick Papers* as "trash."
However, Carlyle and Dickens shared an interest in social reform; their
mutual concern helped to cement this unlikely friendship. Dickens dedicated *Hard Times for These Times*, a commentary on effects of the
Industrial Revolution on the working poor, to Carlyle. Carlyle was the
author of *The History of the French Revolution*, published in 1837; he
later provided Dickens with material that assisted Dickens in writing *A
Tale of Two Cities*. Carlyle's later anti-democratic opinions, especially his
conclusion that the ideal leader is the "Strong Just Man," a forerunner of
Fascist ideology, did not coincide with Dickens's views. Nevertheless,
their friendship endured despite this clash of ideas.

49] Dr. John Elliotson. Autograph letter signed, undated, to "Sir."

In 1844, Dickens decided to aid a carpenter, John Overs, who in Dickens's opinion had shown some literary ability. Overs suffered from
tuberculosis, was unable to work, and as a result he and his family
became destitute. On Dickens's advice, Overs collected what he had
written into a small volume, and Dickens wrote the preface and introduction. Overs dedicated his book, entitled *Evenings of a Working Man*
and published in 1844, to Dr. Elliotson in gratitude for treatment
received free of charge. Dr. Elliotson was also a friend of Dickens and
Thackeray. He saved Thackeray's life during a severe illness, and in gratitude Thackeray dedicated *The History of Pendennis* to him. Dr. Elliotson was the inspiration for the doctor in *Little Dorrit*, and his daughter
inspired Dickens as the prototype for Esther Sommerson in *Bleak
House*. Elliotson was one of the early proponents of "Mesmerism," and
under his tutelage Dickens became an accomplished hypnotist. He practiced this art on friends and members of his family.

50] C. Hare Townshend. Undated engraving, from a photograph.

Dickens dedicated *Great Expectations* to Townshend, who greatly admired Dickens's work. While Dickens was on his second American tour,
his friend Townshend died, leaving Dickens a legacy of £1000 and an
appointment as his literary executor. After much work assembling
Townshend's notes, Dickens had Chapman and Hall publish the com-

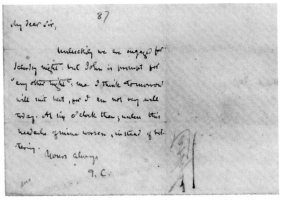

NO. 47   NO. 48

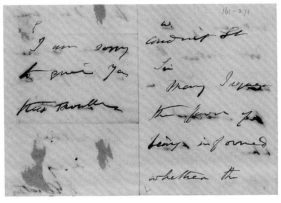

NO. 49   NO. 50

pleted volume, entitled *Religious Opinions of the Late Reverend Chauncy Hare Townshend, Published as Directed in His Will by His Literary Executor.* Dickens provided an unsigned preliminary introduction and edited the text. The book is one of the rarest items in the Dickens canon. The copy exhibited with this portrait of Townshend is a first edition, dated 1869 and except for the introduction and first twenty-five pages, is entirely unopened. Perhaps a copy with unopened pages is not unusual, as jokesters among Dickens enthusiasts insist they have never known of anyone who has read the book through in its entirety!

51] Lady Blessington. Undated publication (originally in *Fraser's Magazine*, 1833) of a drawing by Alfred Croquis (pen name of Daniel Maclise). London: James Fraser.

The portrait is entitled "Author of 'Conversations with Lord Byron,'" and carries the facsimile signature of Lady Blessington. Lady Blessington was the editor of *The Keepsake*, a fashionable annual. In 1844, Dickens contributed a poem "A Word in Season" to it. In 1852, Dickens contributed "To Be Read at Dusk" to the annual (then edited by Lady Blessington's niece, Marguerite Power).

52] Alfred D'Orsay. Undated publication (originally in *Fraser's Magazine*, 1834) of a drawing initialed "A.C." London: James Fraser.

The portrait is unsigned, but the drawing is a companion picture to that of Lady Blessington, and the artist is Daniel Maclise. The portrait is entitled "Author of 'A Journal.'" Count Alfred D'Orsay and Lady Blessington were leaders of the "Gore House Set," a group of intellectuals and

NO. 51   NO. 52

persons of fashion who set standards of culture and taste for the period. Dickens became a member of this group. Edgar Johnson, biographer of Dickens, writes that the dandified appearance affected by Dickens was modeled after Count D'Orsay. Lady Blessington and Count D'Orsay, while not married, lived together. Except for gambling winnings, D'Orsay had no real means of support. When the demand for Lady Blessington's books declined, and her inheritance was gone, the couple fell on hard times. Their extravagant lifestyle came to an end, and Gore House was sold at auction. Lady Blessington and Count D'Orsay moved to Paris in 1849, where Lady Blessington died shortly thereafter. D'Orsay lived until 1852. Victorian moralists must have considered this end of the "Gore House Set" a proper comeuppance.

53] Alfred D'Orsay. Autograph letter signed, [March?] 27, 1841, to (in translation) "Dear Mr. Sainsbur[g?]."

The letter refers to several members of the Petersbourg royalty and discusses the disposition of an unidentified collection.

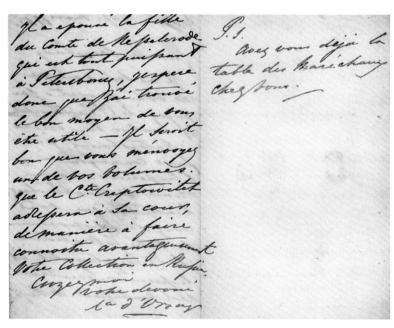

54] William Makepeace Thackeray. Undated engraving.

Thackeray was acquainted with Dickens very early in the latter's career as a novelist. Thackeray, artist as well as novelist, had hoped to be the illustrator for *Pickwick Papers*. He submitted sketches which were rejected by Dickens, much to Thackeray's disappointment and chagrin. Thereafter, the two men were outwardly friendly, but nonetheless rivals. Dickens and Thackeray met socially and Thackeray's daughters were entertained by Katie and Mamie Dickens in the Dickens home. However, at the height of Dickens's marital difficulties, and shortly after Dickens had published the "Personal Statement" in *Household Words*, Thackeray made an unfortu-

nate blunder. Gossip had it that Dickens was involved with Georgina Hogarth rather than Ellen Ternan. Going into the Garrick Club, Thackeray heard the rumor. According to Dickens's biographer Edgar Johnson, Thackeray announced "No such thing – it's with an actress." Dickens was furious and unforgiving. The Dickens-Thackeray friendship had ended. Enter Edmund Yates.

55] Edmund Yates. Autograph letter signed, undated, to "My Dear Lawrence." Mounted with an undated reproduction of a photograph of Yates.

A letter of apology, written apparently as the result of a misunderstanding regarding an appointment. Edmund Yates was a longtime friend of Charles Dickens. He was intimately acquainted with Dickens's personal affairs and had advised Dickens, unsuccessfully, not to publish the "Personal Statement." Yates was an occasional contributor to *Town Talk*, a weekly journal that specialized in publishing critical literary reviews, as well as gossipy, scandalous and libelous comments about prominent figures of the day. Shortly after the appearance of the "Personal Statement" and Thackeray's unfortunate blunder on entering the Garrick Club, Yates selected Thackeray as the subject of his weekly column in *Town Talk*. Yates wrote a scathing article attacking Thackeray's literary ability, personal traits, and character, which Yates considered to be devious and self-serving. Thackeray was furious. However, instead of brushing the article off as the work of a young gossip columnist, Thackeray decided to do battle. Then the whole controversy quickly got out of control. Dickens, Thackeray and Yates were all members of the Garrick Club. Thackeray demanded an apology from Yates, and when Yates did not respond in terms satisfactory to Thackeray, Thackeray placed the whole matter before the membership committee of the club. He claimed, among other charges, that matters discussed by members within the club should stay within it, and not be written about in the press. Yates appealed to his friend Dickens, who wrote letters to Thackeray and letters supporting Yates to the committee. However, neither Thackeray nor the committee would relent and Yates was expelled from the club, his name being erased from the roll of members. Thackeray assumed that Dickens had helped Yates in writing the article in *Town Talk* (he had not). Dickens decided never to enter the Garrick again. Thackeray had won the battle and Yates had been expelled. However, the controversy had severed Thackeray's relationship with Dickens and this estrangement would continue until a few weeks before Thackeray's death.

NO. 55

56] Edmund Yates. Mr. Thackeray, Mr. Yates, and the Garrick Club. [London:] Printed for Private Circulation [Taylor and Greening], 1859.

In his *Bibliography,* Eckel under the chapter "Some Costly Dickensiana" lists this rare pamphlet. Issued by Edmund Yates in 1859, it gives his side of the quarrel between Dickens and Thackeray. This is a copy of the first issue, having "Dickens" misspelled as "Dickes" on page 14. The copy exhibited in the Dickens exhibition held at the Grolier Club in 1913 was also of the first issue.

57] Original front wrapper for *The Cornhill Magazine,* No. 50. London: Smith, Elder and Co., 1864.

Despite her father's estrangement from William Thackeray, Katie Dickens had remained on friendly terms with Thackeray. Several Dickens scholars, including Edgar Johnson and J. W. T. Ley, relate how Katie was instrumental in bringing about a reconciliation between Thackeray and Dickens. Katie prevailed upon Thackeray to make the overture, and it is presumed that she spoke to her father, asking Dickens to accept Thackeray's hand of friendship. Shortly thereafter, Thackeray encountered Dickens in the hall of the Athenaeum Club. Thackeray approached Dickens saying: "It is time this silly estrangement should cease and that we should be to each other what we used to be. Come, shake hands!" Dickens held out his hand and Thackeray took it. Later Thackeray told Katie, "Your father grasped it very cordially and we are friends again, thank God!" Little more than a week later, on Christmas Eve 1863, Thackeray was dead, having suffered a stroke. On learning of Thackeray's death, Dickens in a breaking voice told his friend Marcus Stone the news. Stone replied that he knew how Dickens must feel, as he and Thackeray had not been on friendly terms. Dickens replied "Thank God, my boy, we were." At the request of Thackeray's friends and associates, Dickens wrote "In Memoriam," which was published in the February 1864 issue of *The Cornhill Magazine,* the magazine Thackeray had founded.

58] Page 130, the first page of "In Memoriam" from *The Cornhill Magazine,* No. 50. London: Smith, Elder and Co., 1864.

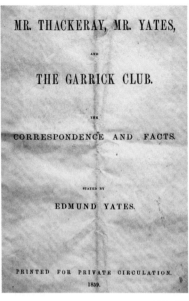

NO. 56   NO. 57

NO. 58   NO. 59

59] John Dickens. Undated portrait of Charles Dickens's father, after a painting by John W. Gilbert and once owned by Henry Fielding Dickens, son of Charles Dickens.

Charles Dickens is said to have dictated most of the changes and modifications to *Memoirs of Joseph Grimaldi* to his father. John Dickens was convivial and unselfish, but also improvident and a spendthrift. These traits of character are also those of Mr. Micawber in Dickens's autobiographical novel, *David Copperfield*. John Dickens's tendency to live beyond his income brought him and his growing family into poorer and poorer circumstances, and led to John Dickens's eventual imprisonment in the Marshalsea. Charles Dickens was only twelve when his father withdrew him from school and sent him to work in a blacking warehouse. There, for a few shillings a day Charles filled bottles with blacking used to polish boots and shoes. Then, John Dickens's mother died leaving him a legacy of £450, which was more than enough to pay his debts and gain his release. Charles quit the blacking warehouse and went back to school. But this was not the end of John Dickens's troubles. He could not hold a job, and he was threatened again and again with imprisonment for his debts (and actually jailed once before Charles could pay for his release). Charles Dickens, having become famous, aided his father financially until the latter's death. In 1834 Dickens wrote to his friend Henry Kolle that John Dickens's troubles were the "damnable shadow cast over my life." However, upon his father's death many years later, Charles remembered his father's convivial spirits, kindness, and unselfishness. Indeed, John Dickens was Mr. Micawber.

60] Catherine Hogarth Dickens. Undated portrait after the painting by Daniel Maclise, circa 1846, and once owned by Kate Perugini, daughter of Charles Dickens.

When Catherine Hogarth married Charles Dickens she was twenty-one and Charles was twenty-four. She was "pleasingly plump" and generally of a cheerful disposition; however, she was inclined to be petulant and at times moody. Charles on the other hand was always full of high spirits, loving but flirtatious. He flirted with Mary Boyle, with whom he

played in amateur theatricals. He flirted with Madame DeLarue, on whom he practiced his art of hypnotism. Catherine objected strenuously to the connection with Madame DeLarue, but Dickens refused to break off the relationship. Catherine's sister Georgina had taken care of the Dickens children while Catherine and Charles were abroad. The children loved Georgina, and in 1842 she became a permanent member of the Dickens household. Catherine soon became jealous of her sister. In the 1850s it became increasingly clear that Catherine was suffering from a nervous ailment. She was subject to periods of confusion and she grew awkward and clumsy. Georgina was forced to assume management of the household. At first, Charles sought to make light of Catherine's difficulties. While she made every effort to please him, he became increasingly irritated with her and the inevitable happened. He moved into a separate bedroom and their estrangement became permanent.

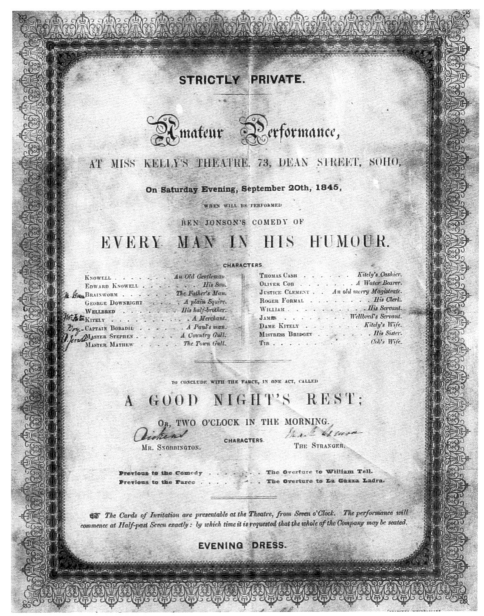

STRICTLY PRIVATE.

Amateur Performance,

AT MISS KELLY'S THEATRE, 73, DEAN STREET, SOHO,

On Saturday Evening, September 20th, 1845,

WHEN WILL BE PERFORMED

BEN JONSON'S COMEDY OF

EVERY MAN IN HIS HUMOUR.

CHARACTERS

KNOWELL . . . . An Old Gentleman.
EDWARD KNOWELL . . . . His Son.
BRAINWORM . . . . The Father's Man.
GEORGE DOWNRIGHT . . . . A plain Squire.
WELLBRED . . . . His half-brother.
KITELY . . . . A Merchant.
CAPTAIN BOBADIL . . . . . A Paul's man.
MASTER STEPHEN . . . . . A Country Gull.
MASTER MATHEW . . . . The Town Gull.

THOMAS CASH . . . . Kitely's Cashier.
OLIVER COB . . . . A Water Bearer.
JUSTICE CLEMENT . . An old merry Magistrate.
ROGER FORMAL . . . . His Clerk.
WILLIAM . . . . His Servant.
JAMES . . . . Wellbred's Servant.
DAME KITELY . . . . Kitely's Wife.
MISTRESS BRIDGET . . . . His Sister.
TIB . . . . Cob's Wife.

TO CONCLUDE WITH THE FARCE, IN ONE ACT, CALLED

A GOOD NIGHT'S REST;

OR, TWO O'CLOCK IN THE MORNING.

CHARACTERS.

MR. SNOBBINGTON. THE STRANGER.

Previous to the Comedy . . . . The Overture to William Tell.
Previous to the Farce . . . . . The Overture to La Gazza Ladra.

The Cards of Invitation are presentable at the Theatre, from Seven o'Clock. The performance will commence at Half-past Seven exactly: by which time it is requested that the whole of the Company may be seated.

EVENING DRESS.

61] [Playbill] Miss Kelly's Theatre, Soho: September 20, 1845. Announcing a performance of *Every Man in His Humour.*

Charles Dickens dominated his wife Catherine, and despite her clumsiness and reluctance to act in his private theatricals, insisted that she perform. She acted in Ben Jonson's comedy *Every Man in His Humour,* having the minor role of Tib, with thirty lines. While it is unlikely that she was in the performance advertised by this playbill, we know that she rehearsed for *Every Man in His Humour* in 1858. During rehearsal, she clumsily fell through the trap door in the stage, injuring her ankle. She was replaced by another actress. Of the cast members in this playbill, Charles Dickens played Captain Bobadil, John Forster played Kitely, and Douglas Jerrold played Master Stephen. Augustus Dickens, Mark Lemon, and the illustrators Frank Stone and John Leech were also in the cast.

62] Charles Dickens. The "Personal Statement" in the June 12 number of *Household Words.* London: Office, 16, Wellington Street North, 1858.

After Catherine's accident while rehearsing for *Every Man in His Humour,* there was a quick succession of events. Dickens purchased a bracelet for the actress Ellen Ternan. The jeweler delivered it by mistake to Catherine. Angry recriminations followed, and Dickens quickly assumed the role of the injured party, protesting that his relationship with Ellen was innocent. Dickens insisted that Catherine call on Ellen and her mother. Catherine tearfully complied, and dominated by Dickens to the end, suffered the indignity of calling on Charles's mistress. Catherine went home to her mother, who began to spread the word to family and friends how Catherine had been abused. Dickens then published the "Personal Statement" in the Saturday, June 12, 1858 issue of *Household Words.* The "Statement" was widely reprinted by newspapers in Britain and America. As if this weren't enough, Dickens then published a statement in the *New York Tribune* of August 16, 1858, in which he again proclaimed his innocence. A footnote to the August 16 article states that Dickens forced Catherine's mother and sister to sign a declaration (obviously written by Dickens) stating that any rumors about Dickens's moral character were untrue and that they now disbelieved such rumors. It has been said that they were forced to sign because Dickens threatened to cut Catherine off without a penny unless they complied. Catherine is a tragic figure in the story of Charles Dickens's life.

63] Mary Hogarth. Undated reproduction of a Hablot K. Browne oil painting, once owned by Georgina Hogarth, Charles Dickens's sister-in-law.

Mary Hogarth, the younger sister of Dickens's wife Catherine Hogarth, lived with Catherine and Charles Dickens until her untimely death in 1836. One evening, Charles and Catherine heard a choking cry from Mary, who then quickly died in Dickens's arms. Dickens was so affected by Mary's death that he suspended his writing of *Pickwick Papers,* composed the writing on Mary's headstone, and is said to have wished to be buried in the same grave with Mary. In a letter to Mrs. Hogarth (Mary and Catherine's mother), Dickens wrote " . . . after she [Mary] died, I dreamed of her every night for many months." Mary Hogarth's death also influenced Dickens's writing of *The Old Curiosity Shop.* According to Edgar Johnson and John Forster, two of Dickens's biographers, Dickens delayed the planned death of the character Little Nell because he felt such anguish over Mary's death. Further, according to Johnson, it was Dickens's original intention in *Oliver Twist* to have his character Rose Maylie die. However, Dickens kept Rose alive, as he could not bear to describe her death in the book. The circumstances surrounding the relationship between Dickens, Catherine and Mary are unclear but nonetheless, rumors and suppositions were widespread during Dickens's lifetime. Some did conclude: "Where there is smoke, there is fire!"

64] Maria Beadnell. Undated reproduction of a photograph.

In the chapter "Some Costly Dickensiana," Eckel lists the *Beadnell and Kolle Letters.* These letters were printed in two books, published by the Bibliophile Society of Boston. The first book is entitled *Charles Dickens and Maria Beadnell; Private Correspondence;* and the second, *The Earliest Letters of Charles Dickens Written to His Friend Henry Kolle.* The volumes are dated 1908 and 1910, respectively. The letters are concerned principally with the relations between Dickens and Maria Beadnell, his

NO. 62

NO. 63

NO. 64

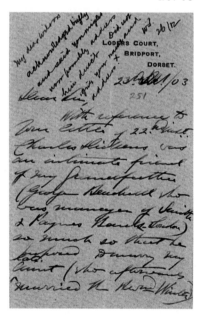

NO. 65

first love. Details regarding this relationship are explained by Edgar Johnson in his Dickens biography. In the mid-1830s, Dickens was a struggling young court reporter. Maria's father was a successful banker. Dickens's friend, Henry Kolle, a bank clerk, was engaged to Maria Beadnell's sister Anne. Through Kolle, Dickens became an intimate of the Beadnell family, was invited to dinners, and to other social occasions. He became thoroughly enamored with Maria, who was pretty, flirtatious, and had a merry laugh. Dickens found her charming. However, Maria's family believed Dickens to be an undesirable suitor, and the affair was eventually broken off by Maria. Over twenty years later, Maria (now Mrs. Henry Winter), the wife of a successful merchant and the mother of two daughters, wrote to Dickens desiring a meeting. Dickens instructed his wife Catherine to call on Maria and invite her and her husband to a private dinner. This dinner was a disaster. Dickens found Maria, now in her forties, to be fat and dull. He found her attempt to seem again flirtatious, absurd. He also discovered that her merry laugh had now become a "silly giggle." Also, Maria had a cold, which Dickens caught. He rebuffed Maria's later attempts to renew the relationship, and broke it off completely.

65] A. G. S. Beadnell. Autograph letter signed, 1903, to "Dear Sir."
The recipient of the three-page letter was apparently inquiring on behalf of a third party. The letter reads in part: "With reference to your letter of the 22nd, Charles Dickens was an intimate friend of my Grandfather (George Beadnell, who was manager of Smith and Paynes Bank-London) so much so that he proposed [to] my late aunt (who afterward married Mr. Henry Winter)." Major Beadnell goes on to say that owing to her coming marriage to Winter, Maria decided not to further entertain Dickens's suit, and writes: "Mr. Kolle and my father were related, exactly how I don't know." Beadnell adds that if the addressee's friend wishes to inform him of his interest in the matter, he will endeavor to help him. The letter was apparently forwarded by the addressee, who has written in the margin: "My Dear Wilson acknowledged briefly and said you might now possibly address him direct. Did not give your name and address. Said you had not already written to him in consequence of indisposition!" In still another hand, there is written in pencil "Alfred George Stubblefield

NO. 66   NO. 67

Beadnell, late King's Own Scottish Borderers. Born 1850, retired 1891. There is a Major A H. M. Beadnell in the Army List, as belonging to the third Battalion, Royal English Fusiliers serving in the 'Provisional Battalion'? His son." It would appear that the unknown "Addressee" was also interested in investigating the Dickens-Beadnell relationship.

66] Ellen Ternan. Undated reproduction of a photograph taken circa 1857.

By courtesy of the Dickens House Museum, London

67] [Illustration] Undated engraving of a scene from *The Frozen Deep*, performed in 1857 by the Guild of Literature and Art in private theatricals at Tavistock House.

This play, originally written by Wilkie Collins, was modified substantially by Dickens in rehearsal, and featured Dickens as producer, director, and actor in a leading role. The play was in part an answer to the charges of cannibalism leveled at lost polar expedition leader Sir John Franklin. The play earned the compliments of Queen Victoria. Dickens decided to take his Company of Strolling Players on the road, and arranged to stage performances in Manchester in August 1857. Up to this time, the cast of *The Frozen Deep* had consisted of Dickens's friends and members of his family. However, Dickens decided that professional actresses should now take the female parts. Three of these roles were then filled by an acting family, the Ternans: mother Frances, and two daughters, Maria and Ellen. Dickens and Ellen performing together in

The Frozen Deep marked the beginning of a relationship that would develop into a notorious liaison. When they first met in 1857, Ellen was eighteen, and Dickens forty-five.

68] [Playbill] Free Trade Hall, reproduction of the original playbill announcing a performance of *The Frozen Deep*, Manchester: A. Ireland and Co., August 24, 1857. By courtesy of the Manchester City Council, Department of Libraries and Theaters.

Charles Dickens is in the cast as Richard Wardour, and Ellen Ternan plays Lucy Crayford.

69] Original front wrapper, designed by Marcus Stone, for Part 4 of *Our Mutual Friend*. London: Chapman and Hall, 1864.

The serial publication of *Our Mutual Friend* was almost interrupted by the Staplehurst Railway disaster, in which ten people died and over forty were injured. While writing *Our Mutual Friend*, Dickens, needing a short vacation, visited Paris. Upon returning, he was accompanied by Ellen Ternan. After crossing the channel, the two boarded the train for the trip to London. Near Staplehurst, rails were being replaced, and the train derailed, catapulting the forward carriages into a streambed. The car in which Dickens and Ellen were riding was tilted precariously over the streambed. Dickens climbed through the window, obtained keys to the carriage doors, and freed Ellen and other passengers. He then went to the aid of the injured and dying. Then, remembering that he had left the manuscript of the next serial number of *Our Mutual Friend* in the compartment, Dickens climbed back through the door and retrieved the manuscript. Dickens was understandably shaken by the incident, and thereafter found it difficult to travel by rail. His efforts to assist the injured were reported in the press and widely commended.

70] W. H. Wills. Undated reproduction of a photograph.

Wills had a one-eighth ownership interest in *Household Words*, the periodical edited by Dickens during the period from 1850 to 1859. Wills also acted as assistant editor of this periodical. Ada Nisbet, in her book *Dickens and Ellen Ternan*, published by the University of California Press in 1952, expands upon the relationship between Dickens and Wills. Prior to

IN REMEMBRANCE OF THE LATE MR. DOUGLAS JERROLD.

FREE TRADE HALL.

UNDER THE MANAGEMENT OF MR. CHARLES DICKENS.

ON MONDAY EVENING, AUG. 24th, 1857,

AT SEVEN O'CLOCK EXACTLY,
(By ten minutes before which time the whole audience is respectfully and particularly requested to be seated),

Will be presented an entirely New Romantic Drama, in Three Acts, by

MR. WILKIE COLLINS,

CALLED

THE FROZEN DEEP.

The Overture composed expressly for this Piece by Mr. FRANCESCO BERGER, who will conduct the Orchestra.

The Dresses by MESSRS. NATHAN, of Titchbourne-street, Haymarket, and MISS WILKINS, of Carburton-street, Fitzroy Square. Perruquier, MR. WILSON, of the Strand.

CAPTAIN EBSWORTH	...	(of the " Sea Mew")				MR. EDWARD PIGOTT.
CAPTAIN HELDING...	...	(of the " Wanderer")			...	MR. ALFRED DICKENS.
LIEUTENANT CRAYFORD	...	...	...	...	...	MR. MARK LEMON.
FRANK ALDERSLEY ...	...	...	...	...	...	MR. WILKIE COLLINS.
RICHARD WARDOUR	...	...	...	...	...	MR. CHARLES DICKENS.
LIEUTENANT STEVENTON	...	...	...	...	...	MR. YOUNG CHARLES.
JOHN WANT ...	...	(Ship's Cook)	...	...	...	MR. AUGUSTUS EGG.
BATESON	}	.(two of the "Sea-Mew's" people)	...		{	MR. SHIRLEY BROOKS.
DARKER	}				{	MR. CHARLES COLLINS.

(OFFICERS AND CREWS OF THE " SEA-MEW" AND " WANDERER."

MRS. STEVENTON	...	...	...	...	...	MRS. GEORGE VINING.
ROSE EBSWORTH	...	...	...	...	...	MISS ELLEN SABINE.
LUCY CRAYFORD	...	...	...	...	...	MISS ELLEN TERNAN.
CLARA BURNHAM	...	...	...	...	...	MISS MARIA TERNAN.
NURSE ESTHER	...	...	...	...	...	MRS. TERNAN.
MAID ...	...	...	...	...	...	MISS MEWTE.

The Scenery and Scenic Effects of the First Act, by MR. TELBIN.
The Scenery and Scenic Effects of the Second and Third Acts, by MR. STANFIELD, R.A., assisted by Mr. CUTHBERT.

At the end of the Play, a Quarter of an Hour's interval for Refreshments.

To conclude with MR. BUCKSTONE'S Farce,

UNCLE JOHN.

NEPHEW HAWK	...	...	...	...	...	MR. WILKIE COLLINS.
EDWARD EASEL	...	...	...	...	...	MR. LUARD.
UNCLE JOHN	...	...	...	...	...	MR. CHARLES DICKENS.
FRIEND THOMAS	...	...	...	...	...	MR. MARK LEMON.
ANDREW	...	...	...	...	...	MR. YOUNG CHARLES.
NIECE HAWK	...	...	...	...	...	MISS MARIA TERNAN.
ELIZA	...	...	...	...	...	MISS ELLEN TERNAN.
MRS. COMFORT	...	...	...	...	...	MRS. TERNAN.

TERMINATING WITH A DANCE BY THE CHARACTERS.

THIS LAST REPRESENTATION taking place, WITH THE VERY LIBERAL CONCURRENCE OF THE FREE TRADE HALL PROPRIETORS, in consequence of the overflows to the two previous performances, and with a careful view to the convenience of a large portion of the Manchester public; the PRICES OF ADMISSION are adjusted as follows:

Stalls (numbered and reserved), 10s.   Private Box Seats, Reserved, 5s.
Galleries and Centre of Hall, 2s. 6d.

AREA OF HALL, ONE SHILLING.

Signed, on behalf of the London Committee,
CHARLES DICKENS, Chairman.
ARTHUR SMITH, Honorary Secretary.

The Office for the Sale of Tickets will be open at the Free Trade Hall, all day on Monday, from 10 a.m. until 5 p.m.

A. IRELAND AND CO., PRINTERS BY STEAM POWER, PALL MALL, MANCHESTER.

NO. 68

Dickens's American tour in 1867 and 1868, Dickens left written instructions with Wills that he was to keep Dickens informed of Ellen Ternan's whereabouts in Italy. Further, Dickens (according to Nisbet's reading of some inked-out diary passages in papers from the Berg Collection) had left coded instructions with Wills that stipulated the conditions under which Ellen was to be brought from Italy to join Dickens in America. However, these conditions were not met, and Ellen stayed in Italy.

71] Georgina Hogarth. Autograph letter signed, March 22, 1913, to B. W. Matz. Mounted with an undated reproduction of a photograph of Hogarth.

Hogarth, Dickens's sister-in-law, resided in the Dickens household from 1842 until Dickens's death in 1870. In this letter, Georgina Hogarth asks Matz, the Dickens scholar, to send "two volumes of the works of C.D – Little Dorrit *and* The Uncommercial Traveller. . . ." Hogarth writes: "You Know I always Give a Book *each* to Two Young Brothers at or about Easter – so I like to have the Books ready to send when the time comes." The letter is signed: "with all best wishes – I am Your's Very sincerely

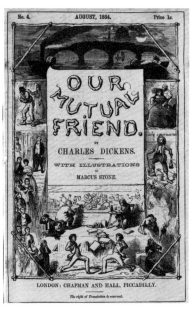

NO. 69   NO. 70

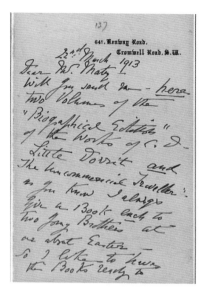

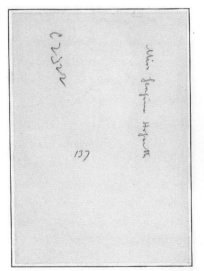

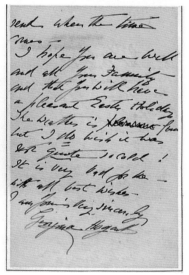

NO. 71

Georgina Hogarth." The manuscript for *A Child's History of England* contains only chapters II and VI in Dickens's hand. The balance of the manuscript was dictated to Georgina. Dickens's wife Catherine was jealous of Georgina, blaming her in part for her own marital difficulties. When Dickens and Catherine separated, their son Charlie Jr. loyally stayed with his mother, while the couple's two daughters, Katie and Mamie, and the remaining sons went to live with Dickens. Georgina also went to live with Dickens. In her will, Catherine made only one bequest to Georgina: a ring cast in the form of a snake! There has been much conjecture about the relationship between Georgina and Charles. There is no doubt that Georgina was a competent manager of the Dickens household, beloved by the children, and a loyal friend and confidant to Charles. She was present when Dickens suffered his last paralytic stroke, ministering to him until the arrival of the doctors. She was there at his death, as was Ellen Ternan. In his will, Dickens left £1000 to Ellen, a large sum in 1870, but certainly not a munificent amount to one who had been his mistress for twelve years or more. He bequeathed to Catherine during her lifetime the annual income from £8000 to be invested by sons Charles Jr. and Henry Fielding Dickens. Again, not an overly generous amount to his wife of 33 years who had borne him nine children. He left all of his personal effects and £8000 outright to Georgina Hogarth!

72] Georgina Hogarth. Autograph letter signed, December 20, 1878, to J. Westland Marston. Mounted with a postmarked envelope addressed to Marston.

Georgina writes that she has returned a letter to Marston, and asks for acknowledgement of its safe receipt. Marston was a close friend of Charles Dickens. In 1842, Marston wrote his first play, *The Patrician's Daughter.* Dickens wrote the prologue to this play. (See Appendix.)

73] Henry Fielding Dickens. Undated reproduction of a photograph originally owned by Georgina Hogarth.

As a child, Henry Fielding Dickens was the editor of *The Gad's Hill Gazette.* Most of Charles Dickens's sons had been a disappointment to him. Alfred and Edward had emigrated to Australia. Augustus had been

NO. 72   NO. 73

employed as a clerk at Chapman and Hall. However, he was financially irresponsible, deserted his wife, and fled to America, where he remained until his death. Charlie failed in several business ventures before his father gave him employment at the offices of *All the Year Round.* Sydney joined the Royal Navy, and while he rose to the rank of lieutenant, Dickens was displeased with his dissipation and financial extravagance. Frank's employment at *All the Year Round* turned out poorly, and he went to India, where he joined the Bengal Mounted Police. Walter went to India in the military service of the East India Company. Later, he served with distinction during the Sepoy mutiny in 1857. Shortly thereafter, Walter became ill and died in Calcutta. Henry Fielding Dickens (pictured here) had a successful career. He went to Cambridge, won a scholarship to the Temple, was called to the bar, and became a successful barrister. In 1928 Henry, now Sir Henry, wrote a book published by Gollancz entitled *Memories of My Father.* In the book Sir Henry, aged eighty, recalls incidents from his childhood.

to Northumberland for a
week until the 27th. On the
28th is my son's wedding day
and on the 29th I go abroad
until the 16th of October when
I shall be back for good

Henry F Dickens

NO. 74

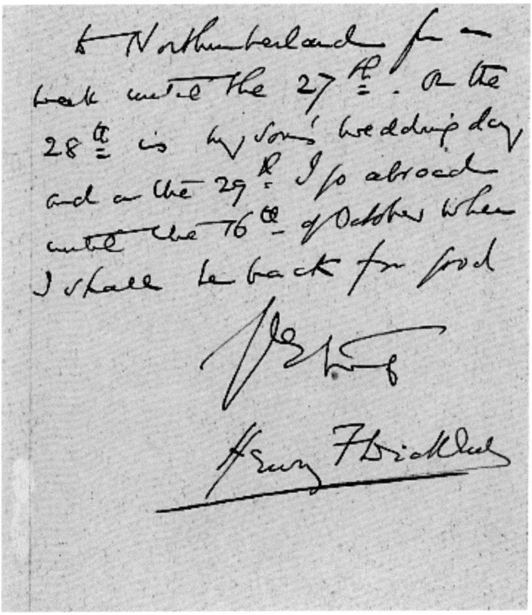

74] Henry Fielding Dickens. Autograph letter signed, September 19, 1904, to B. W. Matz.

The two-page letter comments on the death of their mutual friend, Dickens scholar, F. G. Kitton. Henry Dickens goes on to say that he is going to Northumberland, returning for his son's wedding on September 29, and will be going abroad, returning on October 16.

75] Charles Culliford Boz Dickens. Undated reproduction of a drawing by George Richmond.

Eckel quotes a letter from Dickens to Leigh Hunt, dated July 19, 1842, wherein he promises to send two of Hunt's books to him so that he can personally inscribe them "for the sake of my lawful heir" (Charles Jr., pictured here). This letter also comments on Dickens's quarrel with Colburn over the remittance of the funds due to Mrs. Macrone, who was the beneficiary from the sale of *The Pic Nic Papers*. Eckel quotes the letter in which Dickens writes of Colburn "I damned his eyes." Eckel claims this is the only known letter in which Dickens uses "cuss words."

76] Charles Culliford Boz Dickens. Autograph letter signed, April 12, 1869, to "Sir."

The letter, on "Office of All the Year Round" stationery, reads "I am desired by Mr. Charles Dickens to return you the enclosed but am not charged with any further reply to your letter." This item is presumably a rejection letter concerning an article submitted to *All the Year Round.*

77] Mamie Dickens. Autograph letter signed, March 31, 1887, to "Dear Mr. Kitton."

The letter reads: "The enclosed Photo. is at your service. Be so kind as – when you have done with it to return it to my sister-in-law, Mrs. H. F. Dickens. With kind regards."

78] Mamie Dickens. Undated reproduction of a photograph of a miniature originally owned by Kate Perugini, daughter of Charles Dickens.

Mamie and her sister Kate were the recipients of a copy of *Bleak House* inscribed to them by their father, Charles Dickens. This copy is listed in Eckel's *Bibliography,* in the chapter "Presentation Copies."

CHARLES CULLIFORD BOZ DICKENS,
æt. 15.
From a drawing by George Richmond.

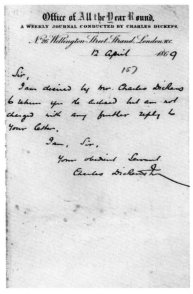

NO. 75   NO. 76

NO. 77

NO. 78

NO. 79

Dear Mr. Shatz

 Only in town for a few hours. So very sorry cannot receive your friends - or I should say *our* friends, - to whom many kind messages. Some day, I hope, when this terrible war is over I may be happy enough to make their acquaintance.

   Very sincerely yours

   Kate Perugini

Aug 25th 1914.

NO. 80

79] Kate Dickens. Undated reproduction of a painting by her husband, C. E. Perugini.

In the chapter "Presentation Copies" in the *Bibliography*, Eckel lists a copy of *Bleak House*, inscribed to his daughters "Mamey and Katie, from their affectionate father."

80] Kate Dickens. Autograph letter signed "Kate Perugini," August 25, 1914, to B. W. Matz.

The letter reads "Only in town for a few hours, So very sorry cannot receive your friends – or, I should say *our* friends, – to whom many kind messages. Some day, I hope, when this terrible war is over I may be happy enough to make their acquaintance." The identities of the friends of Matz, to whom Perugini refers, are a matter of speculation.

81] Original front wrapper for Part No. IX of *The Life and Adventures of Martin Chuzzlewit*. London: Chapman & Hall, 1843.

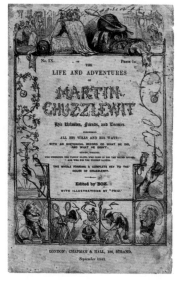

During the publication of this work, Chapman & Hall attempted to reduce Dickens's compensation because the parts were not selling well. Dickens rebelled, and opened negotiations with Bradbury and Evans (this firm advanced Dickens £2400, a one-fourth share for whatever he should write during the ensuing eight years). Direct business relations between Dickens and Chapman and Hall were not resumed until 1858.

82] Original front wrapper for Part XIII of *Little Dorrit*. London: Bradbury and Evans, n.d. [1856].

With the publication of *Little Dorrit*, Dickens's business relations ended with Bradbury and Evans. Bradbury and Evans refused to publish a notice in *Punch* regarding Dickens's marital difficulty with Catherine.

Additionally, Bradbury and Evans had a one-quarter interest in *Household Words*, a periodical edited by Dickens. Upon Dickens's demand, the periodical was discontinued and its place taken by *All the Year Round* under Dickens's sole ownership. Thereafter, Chapman and Hall became Dickens's principal publishers.

83] Title page from Volume III of *The Pic Nic Papers*. By Various Hands. London: Henry Colburn, 1841.

Publication of *The Pic Nic Papers* came about in the following way: John Macrone, who published Dickens's first book, *Sketches by Boz*, drove a hard bargain and Dickens had no further dealings with him. However, when Macrone died, he left a widow and several children in destitute circumstances. Dickens undertook the management of *The Pic Nic Papers*, and decided that the proceeds of the book's sale should go to alleviate the hardship of the Macrone family. Dickens wrote the introduction, and contributed the farce *The Lamplighter's Story*. Other contributors, following Dickens's example, made contributions of stories, essays, etc. also without compensation. Sales of the book realized £300 for the Macrone family. The contents of Volume III started a controversy precipitated by R. Shelton MacKenzie in his 1870 biography of Dickens. It was alleged that the contents of Volume III were annexed from *Charcoal Sketches* by J. C. Neal, and that Dickens had not given proper credit to this source. Dickens stated in a letter to Edmund Yates in 1859 that "of that volume [Volume III] I didn't know, and don't know, anything."

84] Henry Colburn. Autograph letter signed, undated, to "Dear Sir."

In this three-page letter, Colburn criticizes the author's material in volumes one and two of a work on Chateaubriand, which Colburn was apparently publishing. Colburn was the publisher of *The Pic Nic Papers* edited by Dickens in 1841.

85] Hablot K. Browne ("Phiz"). Undated reproduction of a drawn portrait.

"Phiz" supplied the illustrations for all of Dickens's novels (except *Oliver Twist*) beginning with *Pickwick Papers* and ending with *A Tale of Two Cities*.

NO. 82

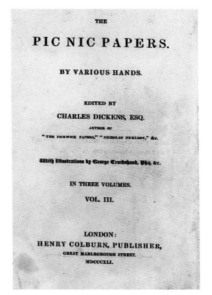

NO. 83

NO. 84

NO. 85

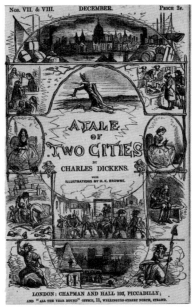 

NO. 86 NO. 87

86] Original front wrapper, designed by "Phiz," for Double Number VII and VIII of *A Tale of Two Cities*. London: Chapman and Hall, n.d. [1859].

With the publication of *A Tale of Two Cities*, Hablot K. Browne's association with Dickens ended. Edgar Browne, in his 1913 biography, *Phiz and Dickens*, states that his "father was suffering declining powers as an artist, and seemed to lose interest in illustrating *A Tale of Two Cities*, many of the plates being carelessly drawn."

87] George Cruikshank. Reproduction of a drawing by F. W. Pailthorpe. London: J. F. Dexter, 1883.

In later years George Cruikshank, once the convivial companion of many in the Dickens circle, became a fanatical teetotaler. This led to the termination of his friendship with Dickens. Mrs. E. M. Ward relates the breaking point in her book *Memories of Ninety Years*, published by Holt in 1926. She writes that at a dinner hosted by Dickens, Cruikshank snatched a wineglass from her hand, intending to dash it to the floor.

This infuriated Dickens, who berated Cruikshank: "How dare you ... it is not for you to object to an innocent glass of sherry!"

88] George Cruikshank. Autograph letter signed, March 31, 1874, to "My dear Sir."

Cruikshank illustrated *Sketches by Boz* and *Oliver Twist*. In this letter, Cruikshank declines an invitation extended to him, on account of his very busy schedule for speaking at upcoming temperance meetings. Cruikshank writes: "I do what I can to promote the Total Abstinence Cause."

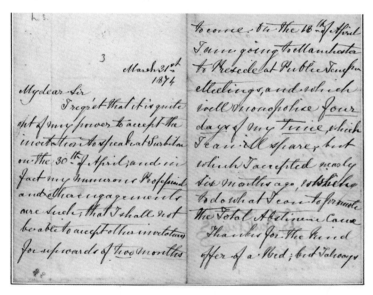

NO. 88

89] [Illustration] Vignette title "The Balloon Sketch" from *Sketches by Boz*. London: Chapman and Hall, 1837.

This illustration, drawn by George Cruikshank, supposedly shows the author (Dickens) and illustrator (Cruikshank) in the basket of the balloon.

90] [Illustration] "Public Dinners" from *Sketches by Boz*. London: Chapman and Hall, 1837.

The publishers (Messrs. Chapman and Hall), the author (Dickens) and the illustrator (Cruikshank) are shown in the drawing.

91] John Leech. Undated engraving.

Leech illustrated *A Christmas Carol* for Charles Dickens.

92] John Leech. Autograph letter signed, undated, to "Dear Professor[?]."

The letter is in regard to the rental of a cottage. Dickens employed many illustrators. His celebrity attracted the prominent artists of the day, who were anxious to have their work appear in a book by him. The list of illustrators includes John Leech, Clarkson Stanfield, Richard Doyle, Daniel Maclise, Sir Edwin Landseer, John Tenniel, F. W. Topham, Richard Seymour, R. W. Buss, Luke Fildes, and R. J. Hammerton.

93] R. W. Buss. Undated reproduction of a portrait.

Buss illustrated Charles Dickens's sketch *A Little Talk about Spring and Sweeps,* which appears in *The Library of Fiction,* published by Chapman and Hall in 1836; a second volume was issued in 1837 but

NO. 90   NO. 91

[handwritten letter — No. 92]

NO. 92

NO. 93

[handwritten letter — No. 94]

NO. 94

contained no Dickens material. *A Little Talk about Spring and Sweeps* was reissued in the Second Series of *Sketches by Boz* in 1836, under the altered title *The First of May.*

94] R. W. Buss. Autograph letter signed, January 26, 1845, to "My dear Henry."

Buss was the illustrator of an early number of *Pickwick Papers* and of one sketch by Charles Dickens for *The Library of Fiction.* A chatty letter, apparently to a close friend, in which Buss complains of an illness and its treatment by a doctor. Buss writes "physician, cure thyself!" He jokingly but affectionately writes that he imagined that he saw Henry's wife Jeannie rising "gradually out of my flowerpots...amidst anemones, etc." He writes that "his blessed book at last at last at last is in the binder's hands" and quotes "life is short, but printing is precious long." Buss says that he has not yet had the two pounds ten shillings interest owed him by a mutual friend.

95] [Illustration] ["The Cricket Match"] from Part Three of *Pickwick Papers.* London: Chapman and Hall, 1836.

The first issue of Part Three of *Pickwick Papers* contains two plates drawn and etched by R. W. Buss, with the page numbers "69" and "74" on them. This item is the first of the two Buss plates, to face page 69 of the text. The two plates, when they appear together in Part Three of *Pickwick Papers* serve as illustration points that distinguish the first issue of this number. Richard Seymour was the first artist selected to illustrate *Pickwick Papers.* However, after completing sketches for only two numbers, Seymour committed suicide; R. W. Buss was selected to replace him.

96] [Illustration] ["Arbour Scene," first issue] from Part Three of *Pickwick Papers*. London: Chapman and Hall, 1836.

This plate is the second of the two Buss plates, to face page 74 of the text, and is the Buss version of the "Arbour Plate."

97] [Illustration] ["Arbour Scene," second issue] from Part Three of *Pickwick Papers*. London: Chapman and Hall, 1836.

The two plates by Buss were unacceptable to Dickens and to Chapman and Hall, who employed Hablot K. Browne ("Phiz") as the illustrator of subsequent parts. This "Phiz" version of the "Arbour Plate" is the first plate drawn by him and was used in lieu of Buss's plate in later issues of Part Three of *Pickwick Papers*.

98] John Tenniel. Undated reproduction of a photograph.

Tenniel designed the frontispiece and vignette title page for *The Haunted Man and the Ghost's Bargain*. In addition, Tenniel designed the four chapter headings. Of the other illustrations, John Leech designed five and Clarkson Stanfield and Frank Stone each designed three. Sir John Tenniel is probably best remembered as the illustrator of Lewis Carroll's *Alice's Adventures in Wonderland* and *Through the Looking Glass*.

99] John Tenniel. Autograph letter signed, March 2, 1880, to George H. Boughton, Esq., A.R.A.

In this two-page letter on mourning stationery, Tenniel declines Boughton's invitation to be his guest at a dinner on May 8, as he has already accepted an earlier invitation to the affair from George Agnew, who "booked me –'like a shot'– very shortly after the dinner last year." Tenniel goes on to say "So you see, 'the early bird *does* pick up the worm'!!!"

100] Richard Doyle. Undated reproduction of a photograph taken by G. Jerrard.

Doyle drew four of the illustrations for *The Chimes*.

101] Richard Doyle. Autograph letter signed, March 6 [n.y.], to "My dear Mr. Cameron" (unidentified).

NO. 96   NO. 97

NO. 98   NO. 99

NO. 100   NO. 101

NO. 102   NO. 103

In this closely written letter, Doyle comments at some length on the fineness of some photographs sent to him by the addressee. He also remarks in part that the photographs are "calculated to drive unfortunate artists to despair and make them throw away brushes and palettes for ever!"

102] George du Maurier. Undated reproduction of a drawn portrait.

George du Maurier was one of the illustrators of Adelaide Proctor's book *Legends and Lyrics.* He wrote *Peter Ibbetson* and *Trilby,* among other works.

103] George du Maurier. Autograph letter signed, April 19 [n.y.], to "Dear Mr[s?]. Browning."

This letter clarifies an appointment to call, and remarks on a past engagement: "What a pleasant evening we had!" In addition to having an introduction by Dickens, Adelaide Proctor's *Legends and Lyrics* is of interest to bibliophiles because it contains du Maurier's work as an artist, which was his principal livelihood before he became a novelist. His novel *Trilby,* which he both wrote and illustrated, was published in 1894 and enjoyed tremendous popularity for a number of years. Readers were charmed by the artist's model Trilby, and the evil Svengali who influenced her. The style of hat worn by Trilby is still referred to as a "Trilby."

104] Charles James Blomfield, Bishop of London. Engraving by William Holl from a bust by Behnes. London: John Murray, 1863.

Sunday Under Three Heads was dedicated by Dickens to the "Right Reverend The Bishop of London." Dickens used the pen name "Timothy Sparks." *Sunday Under Three Heads* was written in 1836 as a protest against a bill introduced in Parliament that would prohibit all work and all recreation on Sunday. The Bishop of London had declaimed against the viciousness of the recreations engaged in by the poor on the Sabbath, and thus tacitly supported the bill. Dickens, therefore, sarcastically dedicated his little political tract to the bishop. *Sunday Under Three Heads* is Dickens's first entry into the social-protest arena. The "poor" against the "rich" would be reflected in a number of Dickens's later works.

105] Charles James Blomfield. Autograph letter signed, August 3 [n.y.], to Frederic Pollock.

A long, chatty two-page letter to a friend, in which Blomfield discusses his sitting for the "fellowship examination," and describes for the addressee the recent activities of numerous mutual friends.

106] Joseph Grimaldi. Undated reproduction of a drawn portrait.

Grimaldi was the subject of Charles Dickens's book *Memoirs of Joseph Grimaldi*, edited by "Boz," and published by Richard Bentley in 1838. A famous clown for whom circus clowns are still nicknamed "Joeys," Grimaldi left an outline of his memoirs, which eventually came into the possession of the publisher Bentley, who gave the manuscript to Dickens for completion and editing. Thus, Dickens edited and wrote portions of the book, although the exact extent of his involvement is unknown.

107] Joseph Grimaldi. Autograph letter signed, July 7, 1831, to Mrs. T. P. Castle.

In this letter, Grimaldi gives instructions apparently clarifying an order for merchandise.

108] J. Westland Marston. Autograph letter signed, April 10, 1884, to Robert Browning.

Marston writes here to Browning, in connection with contributions to the *New Dictionary of National Biography*. Specifically, Marston asks whether it would be agreeable to Browning if he (Marston) wrote the notice of Mrs. [Elizabeth Barrett] Browning. Marston says "I should at least bring to this labour the deepest sense of the nobility and beauty of her poetry, both in spirit and in form and of my deep personal indebtedness to it." Marston goes on to say that his contribution should have the sanction of the addressee.

109] J. Westland Marston. Undated reproduction of a photograph of Marston, taken by J. & C. Watkins.

Marston was the playwright who wrote *The Patrician's Daughter*, for which Charles Dickens wrote the prologue. This play was published in 1841. (See Appendix.)

Ever yours most truly
C. J. London

NO. 104

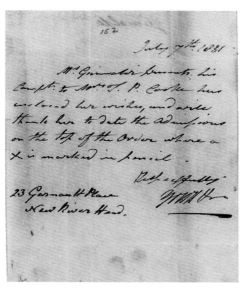

NO. 105

NO. 106

NO. 107

NO. 108   NO. 109

110] Clarkson Stanfield. Autograph letter signed, undated, to "My
dear Colnaghi" [probably Dominic Charles Colnaghi]. Mounted
with an undated reproduction of a photograph of Stanfield,
taken by Watkins and originally owned by Kate Perugini, daughter of Charles Dickens.

The Colnaghi family were proprietors of a well-known gallery engaged in
the sale of old master drawings. Stanfield writes that he is returning two
drawings, having wished that he "could have made them better for you."
He also introduces to Colnaghi a friend, who wishes some advice on a
miniature portrait of Louis XIV. Clarkson Stanfield illustrated a number
of works by Dickens, and upon Stanfield's death, Dickens wrote an article for the June 1, 1867 number of the periodical *All the Year Round*. The
article was entitled "The Late Mr. Stanfield." *All the Year Round* was the
successor to *Household Words* and was edited by Dickens.

111] Dr. Southwood Smith. Undated reproduction of a drawn portrait. [London:] Smith, Elder and Co.

This item and five additional items were apparently collected by Judge

NO. 110

Patterson to extra-illustrate the section on the *Leaflet on Thomas Powell*, included by Eckel in his chapter on "Some Costly Dickensiana." Thomas Powell (eventually revealed as an embezzler and forger) was, according to Dickens biographer Edgar Johnson, originally introduced to Charles Dickens by the latter's ne'er-do-well brother Augustus. Powell and Augustus Dickens were fellow clerks in the office of Thomas Chapman, a friend of Charles Dickens. Through Augustus, Powell ingratiated himself into the Dickens household, and dined several times with Charles Dickens at the Dickens home, Devonshire Terrace. Later, it was revealed that through a series of forgeries, Powell had defrauded his employer (Chapman) out of £10,000! Charles Dickens was informed of this theft in a letter from Thomas Chapman. However, Chapman took pity on Powell for the sake of the latter's family, and forgave his crime. Subsequently, Powell passed forged checks defrauding various tradesmen. He was brought before a magistrate, but escaped prosecution by having himself certified insane and committed to a lunatic asylum, where he was treated by Dr. Southwood Smith. He thereafter fled to New York where he escaped prosecution for another forgery. Powell passed himself off as a literary man who had mingled with many celebrities in London, and he published a sketch of Dickens in *The Evening Post*. Hearing of the sketch, Dickens branded it a "complete and libelous lie." Dickens wrote to New York publisher William Gaylord Clark, giving the latter a full account of Powell's career. Dickens's letter was published in the *New York Tribune*. Powell then sued Dickens for £10,000. In retaliation, Dickens gathered together all of the evidence of Powell's misdeeds, and in 1849 had Bradbury and Evans print these in a four-page pamphlet, which Dickens forwarded to Charles Kent, editor of *The Sun*. Eckel terms this pamphlet the *Leaflet on Thomas Powell*, and says that there is only one known copy of it. Eckel further states that Powell cultivated the acquaintance of various well-known writers, including Leigh Hunt. Robert Browning corrected the proof sheets of a collection of verse published by Powell. According to Eckel, Browning later regretted his acquaintance with Powell, and wrote to a friend, "None of your Powells inspecting my Bowels." According to Eckel, Powell was also acquainted with Tennyson and Wordsworth.

NO. 111   NO. 112

112] Leigh Hunt. Undated reproduction of a drawn portrait, showing Hunt at the age of 66.

Hunt was acquainted with Thomas Powell (See Item 111). Hunt was an essayist, publisher of literary journals, and poet. He had a tempestuous career, once being jailed for two years for libel against the Prince Regent. Despite his success as a writer, he was improvident and constantly in financial difficulties. For the purpose of paying Hunt's debts, Dickens assembled his group of amateur actors and staged several performances of *Every Man in His Humour* for Hunt's benefit. Dickens is said to have modeled the character Harold Skimpole in *Bleak House* after Leigh Hunt. Skimpole, like Hunt, is congenial, vivacious, but unprincipled and constantly in debt.

113] Leigh Hunt. Autograph letter signed, November 5, 1838, to R. H. Horne. Mounted with a franked envelope addressed in Hunt's hand to Horne.

This letter is addressed to fellow writer Horne, and "all who may be in his confidence on the subject." The letter was apparently written after an illness, as Hunt expresses gratitude for the friendship of all those who "have enabled the wounded old bird to sing again."

NO. 113

NO. 114

114] [Illustration] "Halloa, Mrs. Gamp, What are you up to!" Undated reproduction of a drawing by F. W. Pailthorpe.

In his chapter on "Miscellaneous and Unclassified," in the *Bibliography*, Eckel lists *Mrs. Gamp With the Strolling Players*, an unfinished bit of writing that Dickens did in 1847 to aid Leigh Hunt. According to Eckel, it was to be a humorous version of a "New Piljians Projiss." For various reasons, this writing project was discontinued. The first separate publication was done in 1899 from a manuscript owned by Lowell M. Palmer. Only 85 copies were printed. Eckel, in his *Bibliography*, states that the book should be illustrated by a frontispiece portrait of Dickens and by two plates by F. W. Pailthorpe. Oddly, the illustration by Pailthorpe collected here by Judge Patterson is not present in copies of the first edition, although it is similar in style to the plate "Mrs. Gamp's Departure." In the archive plate here, Dickens is pictured in the background, and Cruikshank stands at the left.

NO. 115

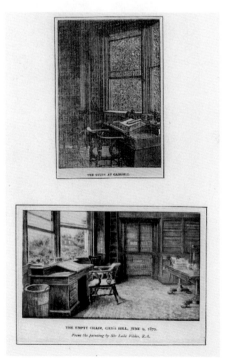

115] [Illustration] "The Study at Gad's Hill." Undated reproduction of a drawing. Mounted with *The Empty Chair, Gad's Hill, June 9, 1870*. Undated reproduction of a painting by Sir Luke Fildes, R.A.

Dickens moved to Gad's Hill Place on March 14, 1856 and resided there until his death on June 9, 1870. The famous Fildes painting was done shortly after Dickens died. Fildes was the illustrator of *The Mystery of Edwin Drood* by Dickens.

116] [Illustration] "The Grave." Undated reproduction of a painting by Sir Luke Fildes. London: Chapman and Hall.

Dickens is buried next to Handel and Macaulay. Nearby are busts of Milton and Spenser, and the monuments to Dryden, Chaucer and Shakespeare.

NO. 116

APPENDIX

The Mystery of The Patrician's Daughter

John C. Eckel in his authoritative bibliography, *The First Editions of Charles Dickens and Their Values*, lists under Part IV – Plays, the "Prologue to *The Patrician's Daughter*." Eckel states that the prologue, written by Dickens and consisting of forty-eight lines, was printed in an octavo pamphlet with paper wrappers and that this was the first edition of the prologue and the play. The play was first performed in December 1842. He goes on to write that the prologue was reprinted in the *Theatrical Journal and Stranger's Guide* for December 17, 1842. He writes that the first edition (the pamphlet with the prologue) is worth, owing mainly to Dickens's contribution, about one pound. Despite the small value of the first edition indicated by Eckel, this first edition he describes has proved to be one of the scarcest items among all of Dickens's works.

During the research and preparation phases of this exhibition of Dickens's life and work, an effort was made to locate a copy of the first edition of *The Patrician's Daughter* with the prologue. In early 2004 a copy offered for sale was inspected. This copy was bound with other 19th century plays. The copy contained a preface but no prologue. Further, a careful collation of the signatures of this work revealed that no pages appeared to be missing or to have been excised. Foxing and ink marks on adjacent pages further corroborated that the play appeared to be complete as issued.

It was then discovered that *Dickens and Dickensiana: A Catalogue of the Richard Gimbel Collection in the Yale University Library*, published in 1980, contained a reference to a copy of an 1842 edition of *The Patrician's Daughter*, and stated that the prologue did not appear in this edition. It became apparent that Eckel had made a mistake and that a copy of the first edition of the play with Dickens's prologue, as described by Eckel, in all likelihood simply doesn't exist.

To complicate matters further the Grolier Club's *Catalogue of the Works of Charles Dickens*, published in 1913, lists "The Original Manuscript of the Prologue (48 lines) which Dickens wrote for Marston's *The Patrician's Daughter*,

1842." However, the Grolier catalogue did not include a copy of a first edition in book form, with the prologue.

Following is a partially conjectured reconstruction of what may have taken place. Westland Marston, a young playwright, wrote the play *The Patrician's Daughter*. Marston was a friend of Charles Dickens and asked Dickens to read the play and give his opinion of it. Dickens liked the play and asked his friend the famous actor William Charles Macready to give a short prologue to be written by Dickens. In a letter dated November 1842, Dickens wrote Macready "[the prologue would] get the curtain up with a dash – and begin the play with a sledge-hammer blow." Macready agreed. Dickens wrote out the forty-eight-line prologue, which he gave to Macready, who recited the prologue at the beginning of performances. Then, Macready may have kept the manuscript or may have given it to John Forster, who was Dickens's literary executor. There is no way of knowing how many hands the manuscript may have gone through between 1842 and 1913, when it appeared at the Grolier exhibition.

However, the following is documented: The prologue was printed in the *Sunday Times* (London) on December 11, 1842. It was then reprinted in the *Theatrical Journal and Stranger's Guide* for December 17, 1842, and in the *Monthly Magazine and Liberal Miscellany* for January 1843. The prologue first appeared in book form as part of Volume One of *The Letters of Charles Dickens Edited by his Sister-In-Law and Eldest Daughter*, published in three volumes by Chapman and Hall, 1880–82.

Apparently John Eckel and Judge Patterson, both Dickens scholars, assumed without ever having inspected a copy that the pamphlet contained the prologue. These facts, and admitted conjecture, are the probable solution to the mystery surrounding the writing, reading, and publication of the prologue to *The Patrician's Daughter*. If not, and an octavo pamphlet with the prologue as described by Eckel should someday turn up, it would certainly be worth more than Eckel's estimate of one pound!

INDEX

Entries refer to catalogue item numbers, not to pages.

525 COPIES PRINTED

TYPESET IN MILLER FONTS

TYPOGRAPHY BY JERRY KELLY